Restoring
the
House of God

Restoring
the
House of God

Dr. Frank M. Reid, III

Treasure House

An Imprint of

Destiny Image® Publishers, Inc.
P.O. Box 310
Shippensburg, PA 17257-0310

"For where your treasure is,
there will your heart be also." Matthew 6:21

ISBN 1-56043-349-3

For Worldwide Distribution
Printed in the U.S.A.

This book and all other Destiny Image, Revival Press, Mercy Place, Fresh Bread, and Treasure House books are available at Christian bookstores and distributors worldwide.

For a U.S. bookstore nearest you, call **1-800-722-6774**.
For more information on foreign distributors, call **717-532-3040**.
Or reach us on the Internet: **http://www.reapernet.com**

Endorsements

"The prolific pen of Dr. Frank M. Reid establishes with eloquence and efficiency a timely and clarion summons to restore the priority of God's presence 'in' the church, as the prerequisite to God's power 'upon' the church, and the authority for societal transformation 'through' the church! It is a must-read for serious minded 'Kingdom' believers."

Bishop Harold Calvin Ray
Senior Pastor, Redemptive Life Fellowship
West Palm Beach, Florida

"Dr. Reid has extended an incredible invitation. It's an invitation to come into our destiny personally and corporately. Come embrace the transforming power of life in Christ for the purpose of extending His Kingdom in our generation. Your children and grandchildren will bless you for it."

Dennis Peacocke
President, Strategic Christian Services
Santa Rosa, California

"In the latter part of the twentieth century, there were many in our world who lost much of the reverence and respect that they used to have for the house of God and the people of God. This I believe is due in part to the attacks of the enemy but is also the result of the failures and shortcomings of persons within the church.

"As we move further into the twenty-first century, it is becoming increasingly important for the Body of Christ to be ever sensitive to the voice of God as He has some powerful plans of restoration, rejuvenation, and inspiration for His Church in this new millennium.

"To this end I commend my friend and brother Dr. Frank M. Reid III, as I believe that he has his hands on the pulse of God with this important, insightful, and timely work, *Restoring the House of God*. I'm convinced that this book will tremendously bless those who read it. It will inspire, inform, educate, and transform the lives and ministries of persons with the wisdom to practice what is taught. It's a must-read!"

Bishop Neil Ellis
Mt. Tabor Full Gospel Baptist Church
Nassau, Bahamas

Contents

Foreword

What can be said of the world today? It's in great deal of chaos. Even the most casual observer sees society's decay before his very eyes. As political, economic, racial and moral issues press in on the tenuous foundations of our world, what lies at the root of this problem is not always clear. It really is the church being lulled to sleep. We have been lulled into compromising in order to get ahead and to get along. We've been tricked into believing political correctness over presenting the truth of the gospel with boldness. We have been placated and patronized into seeking the hand of God over the face of God. We want the things and the blessings but will not push to see Him for who He is over what He can do for us.

There is something desperately wrong, and this is easy to point out. Dr. Reid, however, pointedly describes where the true solution lies. It rests in restoring the house of God. As we move ever so rapidly in the technological revolution, we equally as rapidly are forced away from true relationships, especially with God. This book is a life-changing exposé of biblical figures, contemporary heroes, and a personal witness to help all of us recognize the individual and corporate journey we must take to restore the basic foundations found in Christ.

Dr. Reid points us to the call of God in this day. It is for us to push past the limited and powerless vision steeped in religion and needless tradition into a deeper, intimate relationship with Jesus Christ. It is a call to a worshipful life the elevates us to hear and see God for who He is and then change our lives according to what He is doing. In order to make a difference in the world and perpetuate the Kingdom of God, we need to understand and then embody the spirit, heart, and principles in this book.

I am convinced, and have been for quite some time, that Dr. Frank Reid is a gift to the entire Body of Christ. I respect him as such and embrace him as a covenant friend and son in this awesome move of God. *Restoring the House of God* is a testament to the anointing on his life to change the world through bringing the church back to God's original intent and helping reveal His plan of the Kingdom to us all.

Bishop Eddie L. Long, D.D., D.H.L.
Senior Pastor, New Birth Missionary Baptist Church
Decatur, Georgia

Introduction

With professional precision, but fueled by a preacher's passion, Dr. Frank Reid hands us the buildings blocks for restoring the house of God. He dissects the problem of the headless horseman called the modern church, aimlessly thundering through our cities—powerless to change them. This book challenges the Church to "put your head back on," by restoring the authority of God to the Church.

Dr. Reid starts with restoring the man of God through a personalized retelling of dates with destiny various heroes, both biblical and contemporary, have had. Included is a brief and insightful story of his own journey.

Particularly, I found the chapter regarding "time to clean the house" worth the cost of the book alone. He compromisingly presents such truths as:

> "One reason so much of the house of God is out of order today is because so many of the people of God are 'playing the harlot' with the world...We get all excited for the Lord to touch us and bless up and make us feel good, but we're not interested in living for Him during the week. We want the warmth of feeling without the warfare of faith; the pleasures of the prize without the rigors of the

race. Like spiritual 'junkies' we seek our weekly gospel 'fix' so that we can go back and live like the world the rest of the time. We dress like the world, talk like the world, act like the world, and then wonder why we have no real power in our lives. We 'kiss up' to the world and then complain because we're so miserable.

"Church, it's time to wake up! We've been sleeping with prostitutes! Jesus said that no one can serve two masters. Either we serve God or we serve the world; there is no other option...If we sleep with prostitutes long enough we will get spiritually transmitted diseases. We've got to clean house and break off our 'friendship' with the world. We can't go to 'Bethel' carting around a bunch of 'foreign gods.' "

With writing like this, he clearly defines the difference between entertainment and enlightenment. *We must be enlightened*! This book is a roadmap to restore divine headship. Following the instructions here causes purpose to return, protection to abound, provision to be made, and power to be restored. This book states my heart so well, I wish I had written it! But the next best thing is to have it written by my friend, Frank Reid.

Hand me a brick, Dr. Reid. I'll help you build and restore.

Tommy Tenney
Author and Godchaser

CHAPTER ONE

We've Been Robbed!

On March 10, 1999, the Wednesday evening prayer service had just begun at the New St. John Fellowship Baptist Church in Gonzales, Louisiana when a gunman burst into the room and began firing a semi-automatic pistol into the congregation. In a few moments of shock and terror, the assailant's wife and two-year-old son were killed, along with another worshiper. Four others were wounded. Authorities soon learned that the attacker had also shot his mother-in-law to death outside her home moments before his rampage at the church.

On Wednesday, September 15, 1999, a youth prayer service was just getting underway at the Wedgwood Baptist Church of Fort Worth, Texas when a stranger walked into the foyer at the south entrance of the building. After asking where the prayer meeting was being held, the man pulled out a 9mm semi-automatic pistol and shot three people, killing one. He then proceeded to the sanctuary where he opened fire at random and threw a pipe bomb, which exploded near the pulpit. When police officers arrived, the gunman fatally shot himself in the head. Including the shooter, the final toll was eight dead and eight wounded. Four of the dead were teenagers. The attacker had no apparent connection to the church.

There was a time not too long ago when a church was regarded as a refuge—a safe haven from the violence and corruption of the world. The church was a recognized and appreciated formative influence in the community. Even the irreligious generally respected the moral and spiritual authority of the church. Not anymore.

In recent years the incidences of crime and violence perpetrated on church property and against church people have risen at an alarming rate. Gone are the days when many churches could leave their doors unlocked during the day to serve anyone who might need to come in. Today, more and more congregations are having to confront security concerns. In a recent article, criminologist and crime researcher Paula L. Ratliff described the scope of the problem.

> Church crime is not provincial. It is universal. Acts of vandalism, burglary, arson and violence are taking place inside religious facilities. Houses of worship are being targeted by thieves. Worshipers are being raped, robbed, assaulted and murdered on church grounds.
>
> Estranged husbands and wives are shooting each other during pastoral counseling sessions. Pastors have been assaulted and robbed. People angry with church leadership have driven automobiles through the sanctuary entranceways. Political activists have defaced church property because of anti-abortion and homosexuality stands. Women have been raped when working alone on church grounds and while praying alone in the church sanctuary. Crimes are committed at large and small, urban and rural churches with no established pattern regarding denominational affiliation.[1]

What is the meaning of this disturbing trend, where even worshipers of God can no longer feel safe within the walls of their own churches? I believe it is in part a reflection of the growing moral aimlessness and spiritual emptiness of American society as a whole. In addition, it illustrates the struggle of the contemporary American church to remain relevant in an increasingly materialistic and hedonistic culture. To put it bluntly, the Church is engaged in a culture war.

Culture Clash

Most of us generally give little more than a passing thought to the importance of culture in our lives. For better or for worse, whether good or evil, we are all, for the most part, products of our culture. By culture I mean the customary beliefs, behavioral norms, social forms and customs, material traits and worldview of the racial, religious, or social group from which we derive our primary identity and which shapes our basic philosophy of life. Our attitudes and behavior are influenced not only by our own culture but also by our perceptions of those who come from a different cultural environment.

Life in America today is characterized by an almost continual interaction—often clashing—of different cultures. There is the "white" culture and the "black" culture, the Hispanic culture and the Asian culture. There is the Judeo-Christian culture and the Muslim culture, the Hindu culture and the Buddhist culture. Each of these has unique perspectives and distinctive traits and expectations.

Culture is not limited to ethnic, social, or religious elements, however. It can also be defined by the infrastructure that determines how we live our daily lives. For example, there is the "culture" of the government, the military, the political system, the school system, and the prison system—what we might call the "establishment" culture. Then there is the "street" culture, the culture of the rap artists and the gangs, the drug dealers and the junkies, the pimps and the prostitutes. For many it is a culture of dim hopes and dimmer prospects, an unending grind of fear, anger, addiction, hopelessness, violence, and despair.

One of the major problems we face in America today is that in many places, especially in our cities, the "establishment" culture is not strong enough to deal with the culture of the streets. Consider our urban public schools for example. The "street" culture is pervasive: It determines the clothes our children wear, the language they use, the music they listen to, and their attitude about school.

3

Students who do well are branded "nerds," which is an invitation to abuse and considered a fate worse than death. This is why many smart young men and women deliberately do poorly in school, so they can be affirmed, right where they live, by the culture of the street.

Even in our prisons the "establishment" culture of the correctional system cannot overcome the "street" culture that defines the vast majority of the inmate population. There are gangs in prison; there are drugs in prison; there is rape, sodomy, and murder in prison.

This negative, destructive "street" culture that runs throughout our society is more powerful than the "establishment" culture of our schools, our prisons, and our government; and if we are not careful, it will become more powerful even than the "culture" of the Church itself. The danger signs are everywhere. Many folks out on the street, young people as well as others, have told me that while they believe in God and know they need Jesus in their lives, they feel they cannot take that step. When they are among their own crowd in the culture of the street, to be recognized as a Christian, to be known as a "church" man or woman or boy or girl is to be identified with that which is considered weak and wimpish.

You're Out of Order!

By and large, the American church today is generally ineffective in influencing lives, changing hearts, bringing lost people to Christ, or impacting society for the glory of God. Surely it cannot be the Lord's desire for His Church to be seen by the world as "weak and wimpish." What has happened? Why is the culture of the street threatening to overwhelm the culture of the church in our society? I believe that one of the primary reasons is that the American church today has become largely *dysfunctional*.

I'm not sure if I really like the word *dysfunctional*; it's so clinical. It does, however, define the problem. *Dysfunctional* means impaired or abnormal functioning. We live in a dysfunctional society: Our families are dysfunctional, our marriages are dysfunctional, and our children are dysfunctional. For example, even though Americans are now experiencing the greatest economic prosperity of the last 50 years, we are also facing more internal problems than ever before. Our economy is strong, yet there are just as many poor people as ever. The democratic framework of our nation appears stable and strong, yet internal stresses threaten to tear apart the very fabric of our social order. "Family values" is an important and popular topic these days, but lately the definition of *family* has been broadened to the point where the word has become almost meaningless. Although a strong majority of Americans express belief in God and regard the Bible as the Word of God, most of them live their lives as if these beliefs make no difference.

This cancer of social, moral, and spiritual dysfunctionalism is rooted in the fact that even though we may have good jobs, make good money, have a good education, drive a nice car, own a nice house, and are able to send our children to private schools and academies, when it gets down to the nuts and bolts of everyday life, most of us live lives that are out of order. Because our personal lives are out of order, our churches are out of order. If our churches are out of order, how can they be effective in reaching the lost or promoting a Christ-centered worldview? How can we lead the blind when we can't even see where we are going ourselves?

Many, many churches all across our land, although filled with people and busy with activity, are empty of God's power to change lives and transform communities. Why? The house of God is filled with people who are living in rebellion against the order of God in their lives. God only sends His divine presence and power to a house and a people who are in divine order. Our society and our families are dysfunctional because *the house of God is out of order.* The culture of the street has more influence on people's lives than the culture of the church because *the people of God are out of order.*

King David, the "sweet psalmist of Israel," wrote,

Behold, how good and how pleasant it is for brethren to dwell to-gether in unity! It is like the precious oil upon the head, running down on the beard, the beard of Aaron, running down on the edge of his garments. It is like the dew of Hermon, descending upon the mountains of Zion; for there the Lord commanded the blessing; life forevermore (Psalm 133:1-3).

This is a good picture of divine order. Brothers dwell in unity when the anointing flows from *the head* all the way down. Christ is the Head of the Church. Divine order and structure prevail when we acknowledge and submit to Christ's Headship. The problem is that many of us are afraid of His headship, or rebel against it. We have our own ideas and opinions about how things ought to be and how things should be run. We come together, debate and discuss, and vote on our ideas, but don't take the time to try to find out if we are doing what God wants us to do. When we cut ourselves off from knowing, understanding, or seeking God's will for our church, our family, our job, or whatever, we get out of order. Then we wonder why we have problems with our relationships or our finances, and why there seems to be no spiritual power in our lives or in our congregations. It is because we are out of order.

Blessings, power, prosperity, purpose, and effectiveness depend on the house of God being under the divine order of God. Without that order there is chaos, dysfunction, judgment, impotence, and irrelevance. We need to return to divine order. *It is time to restore the house of God.*

Thief in the Sheepfold

Why does the house of God need to be restored? A thief has quietly crept in and robbed us blind! It has happened so subtly that many Christians and many churches are unaware that anything is wrong. Restoring the house of God means putting back what was taken, reclaiming that which the thief has stolen.

In the tenth chapter of John's Gospel, Jesus speaks of thieves and robbers who try to sneak into the sheepfold, whereas the shepherd enters by the door. As long as the sheep listen to the shepherd and follow him, they will not follow the thief. Jesus said, "The thief does not come except to steal, and to kill, and to destroy. I have come that they may have life, and that they may have it more abundantly. I am the good shepherd" (Jn. 10:10-11a). The house of God needs to be restored because many sheep have stopped listening to the Shepherd and instead are listening to the thief.

Throughout much of the American church the "spirit of religion" has come in and stolen our understanding of what Christ meant the Church to be. By "spirit of religion" I mean a faith that focuses on man rather than God. It means "playing church" and "having a form of godliness but denying its power" (2 Tim. 3:5a). A "religious" spirit is flesh-focused: essentially selfish and worldly. Left unchecked, it will eventually lead to division and destruction. A "religious" spirit seeks entertainment rather than enlightenment, the pleasures of the flesh rather than the power of the Spirit, and the *favors* of God rather than the *face* of God. "Religious" churches, lacking the presence and power of God, try to compensate by substituting programs and practices, form and ritual, tradition and habit. They are "out of order" and have no power or authority to make a real difference in people's lives. "Religious" Christians "worship" for a couple of hours on Sunday and then go back to the secular world and their secular lifestyles, still bound in sin and ignorance.

The "spirit of religion" removes our focus from the face of God and redirects it onto the principles of man. It robs us of our identity, our sense of purpose, and our knowledge of who we are and what we have received in Christ. It also robs us of our Christian joy and confidence. Worst of all, however, a "religious" spirit robs us of our *intimacy with God.*

The Missing Key

True intimacy is an increasingly rare quality in modern American society. It seems as though everything in our culture centers on the quick and convenient. We're always looking for faster ways to do things: fast food, ATMs, E-mail, Internet shopping, and stock trading. One consequence of this hurry-up attitude is a minimizing of face-to-face human contact. Americans today seek freedom without responsibility, choices without consequences, and "love" without commitment. Yet underneath this fast and impersonal façade, millions of Americans are crying out desperately for genuine relationship—for true intimacy.

The same is true in much of the Church. Millions of American Christians live their daily lives, go to church, work their jobs, attend school, and participate in all manner of sports, clubs, or other recreational activities with little or no experience of intimacy with God. They do not have intimacy with God in their daily lives because they don't experience it in their churches.

When was the last time you really felt close to God? How long has it been since you sensed or saw the power and presence of God in your church? Do you know Him intimately? Do you delight to walk by His side day by day? Do you have a relationship with God that brings peace, order, power, and confidence to your life? Intimacy with God is the main thing that the "spirit of religion" has stolen from us. It is the missing key that unlocks divine power to the Church, the foundation upon which discipleship and effective ministry rest.

When we lose our intimacy with God, we lose our sense of divine order. When we lose our sense of divine order, we lose our sense of divine power and presence. When we lose our sense of divine power and presence, we lose our sense of divine peace. When we lose our sense of divine peace, we open ourselves up to all sorts of fears and uncertainties. Our enemy the devil has a strategy. John 10:10 says that the thief comes to steal, kill, and destroy. He begins by stealing our intimacy with God. Once that is taken away, it is easy for the "religious" spirit to come in and steal our family, our children, our joy, our power, and our ability to relate the gospel of Jesus Christ to our communities in a realistic, relevant, and redemptive way.

Satan's ultimate goal is to kill and destroy: destroy our relationships, destroy our witness in the world, destroy our confidence, and even destroy our faith, if possible. Behind the rise in crime and violence on church property, satan tries to tell us, "Because you have no power, I'm coming in to strike fear in the hearts of your worshipers." When we lose our intimacy—our sense of closeness to God—everything else is in danger because everything else is rooted and grounded in that intimacy.

Intimacy with God means walking in a day-by-day, moment-by-moment relationship with God, seeking His face, sensitive to His voice, and submissive to His will. When we walk with the Lord in this way, we can learn His thoughts, know His heart, and see where He is working and what He is doing. His power and presence become very real to us. Walking with God strengthens love and faith and drives out fear, confusion, and disorder. Such intimacy infuses individual Christians as well as churches with courage, confidence, and boldness to aggressively engage the world and the "gates of hell" rather than sit by passively, devoid of power and passion.

Restoring the House

Restoring the house of God means restoring intimacy with God. It means rebuilding the basic foundation of *relationship*. Jesus spoke of this when He said, "I am the door. If anyone enters by Me, he will be saved, and will go in and out and find pasture....I have come that they may have life, and that they may have it more abundantly" (Jn. 10:9–10b). Being saved, going in and out and finding pasture, having abundant life— all of these describe a *relationship* with the "good shepherd." Relationship with God is fundamental; it is the seed from which every other relationship grows: spouse, children, church, workplace, and community. If our relationship with God is out of order, every other relationship we have will be out of order as well.

Christ established the Church and called us to be His representatives on the earth, to preach the good news, and make disciples in all the nations. In order to accomplish that mission, we must be in proper relationship with Christ, who is our Head. Only then can we see and understand the world the way He does and reach that world the way He wants. If we lose our intimacy with Him, we lose our ability to see through His eyes, feel through His heart, and respond to His will. Instead, we dash about from here to there, doing this and that, full of activity, satisfied that we are "serving God" when in reality all we are doing is spinning our wheels, going nowhere fast. This is at the core of our general failure to make any lasting difference in our communities and society. It is the basic reason why the Church has become dysfunctional in American culture.

When we talk about restoring the house of God, we are not talking about restoring an institution as much as we are a worldview. We don't need a "new vision" for a new millennium. We simply need to return to the original vision that God gave us. That vision focuses not so much on the hand of God, the gifts of God, and the blessings of God—all of which are important—but on the *face* of God. Our vision is to be in the *presence* of God, not just to receive "presents" *from* God.

A popular view among many today is that the Church is like a cafeteria or supermarket where each person selects what he wants and passes up everything else. Many people pick and choose their religion or their church in the same way they buy groceries. They try something. If they like it, they stay with it; if they don't like it or it doesn't meet their needs, they try something else. Many churches, having lost their intimacy with God, have ended up catering to this "supermarket" mentality, seeking to draw people in through gimmicks or savvy marketing or by trying to be "socially relevant."

As long as the Church caters to the world, we will never reach the world. If we try to be a "supermarket" for people's needs, all we will succeed in doing is to titillate people for a little while. The mission of the Church is not to titillate but to transform. Until we return to the foundation of intimacy and relationship and restore the Church to the house of God under His divine order, we will not see the spiritual transformation of individuals, communities, and the world by the power of God.

Many churches and individual believers have adopted a passive worldview that sees faith as only a small part of the real world. In such a view, the "church" becomes a powerless and meaningless institution, a religious museum that we visit each Sunday, where we sing our little hymns, pray our little prayers, and then go right back to the same old things we were doing before.

Restoring the house of God will restore to the Church a theo-centric worldview that sees God at the very center of everything. It could also be called a *Kingdom worldview*: God-rooted, Christ-centered, and Holy Spirit-empowered. This worldview puts everything back in order. First, it puts each of us in order with God as individuals. Once we are in order with God, then all of our subsequent relationships fall into order. Out of that order comes structure: family structure, community structure, church structure, governmental structure, economic structure, social structure, cultural structure.

A Kingdom worldview affects how we relate to our culture. It influences (or *should*) what we watch, what we read, and what we listen to, as well as what we let our children watch, read, and listen to. It influences our motivations and level of involvement in trying to change society. The Kingdom worldview will inevitably bring us into conflict and confrontation with the prevailing worldview in our culture. We see it all the time. It goes by many names: culture war, liberal versus conservative, left versus right. No matter what society calls it, in reality the conflict is between the Kingdom of God and the kingdom of this world.

The Time Is Now

It's time to restore the house of God. We need to come under divine order once again and return to intimacy with God.

Josiah was a king of Judah who reigned for 31 years in Jerusalem. The Book of Second Kings describes him as one who "did what was right in the sight of the Lord, and walked in all the ways of his father David; he did not turn aside to the right hand or to the left" (2 Kings 22:2). Josiah reigned over a land and a people who were out of divine order. Many lived in open rebellion against God. Idolatry was widespread and sexual immorality was rampant. The Jews had forgotten God and His law. Their wickedness was so great that God had already pronounced inescapable judgment against the nation.

Motivated by a pure heart that sought to follow God, Josiah initiated spiritual reforms throughout the land, beginning with the cleaning and repair of the Temple, which had fallen into neglect. During the cleaning, a copy of the book of the law was found in the Temple. When it was read to Josiah, the young king was convicted in his heart over the sin and spiritual neglect of the people. He sought the Lord for guidance. God said that the nation would be judged for her great sins, but that because Josiah had sought the Lord, the judgment would be withheld until after his death.

Josiah then pledged anew his devotion to the Lord. He destroyed pagan altars and worship places throughout the land, deposed and executed pagan priests, led the people by example and action to a renewal of faith with repentance and cleansing, and observed a celebration of the Passover that was the greatest and highest in living memory.

One significant act that Josiah performed during this time involved a place called Bethel.

> *Moreover the altar that was at Bethel, and the high place which Jeroboam the son of Nebat, who made Israel sin, had made, both that altar and the high place he broke down; and he burned the high place and crushed it to powder, and burned the wooden image* (2 Kings 23:15).

Bethel means "house of God." Originally a place of divine visitation, Bethel was a sacred place to the Jews, dating back hundreds of years to the days of Jacob. Jeroboam, the first king of the northern kingdom of Israel after the nation divided following the death of King Solomon, erected a pagan altar at Bethel and initiated pagan worship at the site. Bethel, the "house of God," was thus corrupted by the sin of the people and brought out of divine order. By destroying the altar and cleansing the site, Josiah restored the "house of God" at Bethel.

The spirit and actions of King Josiah provide a good example and model for us. We need to restore the house of God. The thief has held what belongs to us long enough. How do we restore the house of God? How do we regain the intimacy that has been taken? The answers to these questions will come as we understand more about what Bethel was and what it represented to the Jews. Once we understand what Bethel represents, God can use this understanding to put our homes in order, our lives in order, and our churches in order. *Let's restore the house of God!*

Endnotes

1. Paula L. Ratliff, "Make Your Church Building Safer," *The Deacon* Winter 1999-2000, Nashville: Lifeway Christian Resources. Quoted in Charles Willis, "Lifeway's *Deacon* magazine focuses on violence at church," Baptist Press, September 17, 1999. 10/8/99 <http://www.sbc.net/articles/1999/0...RL=http://www.sbc.net/bpSearch.asp

CHAPTER TWO

From Vagabond to Visionary

E ven though the boys were twin brothers, they couldn't have been more different. Esau, the firstborn and his father's favorite, was the outdoors type. Husky and hairy, he was never happier than when alone in the wilderness with his bow and arrow, pitting his wits and stealth against an elusive deer. Impulsive to a fault, Esau lived for the moment, giving little thought either to the future or to the long-term consequences of his decisions. The responsibilities of family leadership held little appeal for him.

Jacob, on the other hand, did not care for the rustic life. Preferring the ease and comfort of the tents, Jacob was strictly a homebody and a spoiled mama's boy. Beneath his smooth skin and mild demeanor, however, beat the heart of a born con man. Jacob was a "slickster" and a trickster with the personal philosophy of never *working* for anything that he could get by scheming instead. His fertile mind was ever concocting some plot or another to get what he wanted. Even his very name reflected his character. *Jacob* literally means "heel-catcher," as in one who trips up someone else, referring to how he was born grasping the heel of his twin brother, Esau (see Gen. 25:26). The name also means "supplanter" or "deceiver." All of these are accurate descriptions of this rascal. Jacob was a pampered rich kid with too much idle time on his hands.

To make matters worse, the brothers grew up in a dysfunctional home. "And Isaac loved Esau because he ate of his game, but Rebekah loved Jacob" (Gen. 25:28). Anytime parents show favoritism between their children, there's bound to be trouble. Can you imagine the sibling rivalry that must have existed between Esau and Jacob, as dissimilar as they were and each aware that they were not equally loved by one parent or the other?

Although he was a twin, as the second-born, Jacob could expect to inherit only one-third of his father's estate; the rest would go to Esau. The laws and customs of the day strongly favored the firstborn in a family. Esau was expected to rise to the headship of the family clan upon the death of his father, Isaac. Schemer that he was, Jacob probably found this state of affairs less and less acceptable as he grew older, and began to look for ways to turn circumstances to his own advantage. In this his mother, Rebekah, encouraged him.

Why Rebekah preferred Jacob to Esau is not completely clear. Perhaps it was because Jacob had always stayed so close to home, or because he was the youngest. Perhaps it was because Rebekah remembered the words the Lord had spoken to her shortly before her sons were born. "And the Lord said to her: 'Two nations are in your womb, two peoples shall be separated from your body; one people shall be stronger than the other, and the older shall serve the younger' " (Gen. 25:23). God had announced ahead of time that Jacob would supplant and rise above Esau. Perhaps Rebekah thought she could help God out by encouraging Jacob in his deceptions.

Jacob was the grandson of Abraham, to whom God had promised, "I will make you a great nation; I will bless you and make your name great; and you shall be a blessing. I will bless those who bless you, and I will curse him who curses you; and in you all the families of the earth shall be blessed" (Gen. 12:2-3). In accordance with God's Word, Isaac was born to Abraham in his old age, the son through whom God's promise would be fulfilled. Isaac had only two sons, Esau and Jacob, and Jacob would rise up to rule over his older brother. Clearly, God's plan for raising up a great nation from Abraham's descendants included Jacob, but how would it come about?

What could God possibly do with such a scheming, deceiving trickster as Jacob?

Run for Your Life!

The Book of Genesis records two specific incidents in Jacob's early life that not only reveal his character but also set in motion the sequence of events leading up to his encounter with God. The first is found in Genesis 25:29-34.

One day, as is his custom, Esau goes out hunting. Apparently his skills fail him on this occasion because he comes back empty-handed, tired, and hungry. As he approaches the tents of home he catches a whiff of the mouthwatering aroma of cooking stew. Sure enough, there is Jacob, sitting by a cook-fire, calmly stirring a pot of bubbling, beefy broth. Licking his lips, Esau walks over to Jacob and says, "Listen, man, I'm really tired and hungry. Let me have some of that stew."

Never one to give away *anything* for nothing, Jacob looks up and says, "Okay, but first, sell me your birthright." I wonder how long Jacob had been planning something like this, just waiting for his opportunity! What audacity, to demand his brother's birthright in exchange for a bowl of stew! Yet, Jacob knows his brother. He knows that Esau is quick to act but slow to think, and on this occasion Esau doesn't disappoint him.

"I'm dying of hunger! What good will a birthright be if I'm dead?" Just like that, the transaction is made: Esau gets his stew and Jacob gets the birthright. I can almost imagine Jacob thinking, as he watches Esau wander off with his bowl of stew, *This was too easy!*

Incident number two is recorded in chapter 27 of Genesis. Jacob already owns Esau's birthright. Now, at the instigation of his mother and with her help, he deceives his father in order to obtain for himself the generational blessing that rightfully belongs to Esau as the firstborn.

Isaac is old and blind and apparently fears that his death is near. Desiring to bless his oldest son before dying, Isaac sends Esau to hunt game and "make me savory food, such as I love, and bring it to me that I may eat, that my soul may bless you before I die" (Gen. 27:4).

Overhearing the conversation, Rebekah concocts a scheme with Jacob to claim Isaac's blessing. While Esau is gone, she takes two kids from the flock of goats, prepares "savory food" such as Isaac loves; and Jacob, dressed as Esau, takes the meal to his father and waits there until he receives the blessing. At first, Jacob protests out of fear that if the deception is discovered he will receive a curse from his father instead of a blessing. Jacob's momentary burst of conscience passes, however, and his determined self-interest quickly takes over again. Pushing aside his fears, Jacob goes along with his mother's plan.

Despite a couple of tense moments, the scheme works. Jacob carries the food in to Isaac, who is surprised that Esau has returned so soon. He is also suspicious when he hears what sounds like Jacob's voice. Calling his son closer, Isaac touches him to determine whether it is Esau or Jacob. Fortunately for him, Jacob is wearing Esau's clothes and has goatskins on the smooth parts of his neck and hands, so that he feels hairy like Esau. Isaac is taken in by the deception, and gives Jacob the blessing intended for the firstborn. "Therefore may God give you of the dew of heaven, of the fatness of the earth, and plenty of grain and wine. Let peoples serve you, and nations bow down to you. Be master over your brethren, and let your mother's sons bow down to you. Cursed be everyone who curses you, and blessed be those who bless you!" (Gen. 27:28-29) Afterwards, Jacob loses no time getting out of there, having hardly dared to breathe and scarcely able to believe that he has really pulled it off.

Jacob's relief and self-satisfaction do not last long, however. A sad scene ensues a few minutes later when Esau arrives from the field with food for his father. Isaac is distressed to learn that he has been deceived and has given Esau's blessing to Jacob, but there is nothing he can do. On Esau's part there is weeping and wailing, and begging his father for even one small blessing. In the end, Esau leaves his father's presence nursing a murderous hatred for Jacob. *It won't be long before my father is gone. Then, Jacob's a dead man!*

Hearing of Esau's plan to kill Jacob, Rebekah warns her youngest son to flee his brother's wrath. Jacob knows that the jig is up. He's in real trouble now. Jacob the "heel-catcher" has caught one heel too many, and if he wants to continue breathing, he had better run for his life.

Wayside at the House of God

Jacob departed with haste, but not before receiving final instructions from his parents. Rebekah advised him to go to her brother Laban's home in Haran and stay there "a few days" until Esau's anger cooled (Gen. 27:44). For Jacob the "few days" would become 20 years. Jacob's flight was given some semblance of dignity by attaching to it the purpose of his seeking a wife from among his mother's family. Isaac sent Jacob off with a final blessing that reflected what God had in store. "May God Almighty bless you, and make you fruitful and multiply you, that you may be an assembly of peoples; and give you the blessing of Abraham, to you and your descendants with you, that you may inherit the land in which you are a stranger, which God gave to Abraham" (Gen. 28:3-4).

So, like a vagabond with the road stretched out before him, Jacob left his home and family, armed only with a destination and the generational blessing of the covenant promise passed down to him, through his father, Isaac, from Abraham. Jacob was a man on the run. Little did he know that he was about to run smack into God.

> *Now Jacob went out from Beersheba and went toward Haran. So he came to a certain place and stayed there all night, because the sun had set. And he took one of the stones of that place and put it at his head, and he lay down in that place to sleep* (Genesis 28:10-11).

19

Although God had promised a blessing for Jacob, Jacob had to move out to receive it. As long as he remained in his old home and his old ways, he could not realize the blessing. It would be fulfilled only as he moved forward to claim it. Jacob could not stay where he was and become the man God wanted him to be. The same is true for us. God wants to bless us, but we have to be willing to step out in faith to receive it. We can't insist on staying the way we are and at the same time expect God to bless us. Blessings almost never come while we're sitting in our comfort zones.

Now Jacob probably wasn't thinking about his blessing when he stopped at that "certain place" for the night. He was tired, perhaps hungry, probably scared, and simply wanted to sleep. Jacob wasn't looking for God that night, but God was looking for him. Sometimes God meets us in the most unexpected places and in the most unanticipated ways. To the naked eye there was nothing special about the place where Jacob stopped that night. In fact, it was so barren that the only thing he could find to use as a pillow for his head was a rock!

Perhaps Jacob had time to reflect on the sudden change in his circumstances. After all, it was quite a contrast moving from the pampered son of rich parents to a fleeing fugitive in the wilderness. Sometimes we have to be brought low before we will look up. Yet, as humble and unpromising as his situation appeared, Jacob was right where God wanted him. Unknown to him, Jacob had stopped at the house of God! Before the night was over, his life would be changed forever.

Then he dreamed, and behold, a ladder was set up on the earth, and its top reached to heaven; and there the angels of God were ascending and descending on it. And behold, the Lord stood above it and said: "I am the Lord God of Abraham your father and the God of Isaac; the land on which you lie I will give to you and your descendants. Also your descendants shall be as the dust of the earth; you shall spread abroad to the west and the east, to the north and the south; and in you and in your seed all the families of the earth shall be blessed. Behold, I am with you and will keep you wherever you go, and will bring you back to this land; for I will not leave you until I have done what I have spoken to you." Then Jacob awoke from his sleep and said, "Surely the Lord is in this place, and I did not know it." And he was afraid and said, "How awesome is this place! This is none other than the house of God, and this is the gate of heaven!" (Genesis 28:12-17)

In Hebrew, the "house of God" is *Beth-el*, which is the name that Jacob gave to the place where God met him on the run (see Gen. 28:19). For Jacob, Bethel was a place of divine encounter: a house of vision, a house of voice, and a house of visitation.

Open Your Eyes and See

Jacob had a dream that night unlike any he had ever had before. He saw angels ascending and descending a ladder that reached from the earth to Heaven. It was a powerful vision in which even God Himself appeared to Jacob. When Jacob awoke from his sleep, he was a changed man. His vision gave him a completely new perspective on life, opening his eyes to spiritual realities as never before. Until his night at Bethel, Jacob had been strictly a man of the world, living for his next scheme and always working to advance himself. Certainly Jacob knew *about* God—Isaac and Rebekah had taught him—but he had never *known* God *personally*.

Bethel changed all that. God grabbed Jacob's attention and focused it on new possibilities and wider horizons than his own self-centered view of the world. The vision opened Jacob's imagination and drew him into a *personal encounter* with God. For probably the first time in his life, Jacob realized that the God of Abraham and Isaac was *his* God, too, and that the covenant promise of blessing and fruitfulness that God had given to Abraham and Isaac was meant for him as well. Jacob's vision at Bethel forever altered his destiny, bringing his life into God's order and putting him on the track that God had designed for him to follow.

Proverbs 29:18a (KJV) says, "Where there is no vision, the people perish." Today there are many, many churches and Christians who are "perishing" because they have lost their vision. They have gotten out of God's order and have forgotten how to dream. Can you remember a time when God gave you a vision, a dream of what He wanted you to be or do in Him? Has your church dreamed such a dream? Where is that vision now? Are you living it out day by day, becoming what God has called you to be, or have you slipped back into your old ways and old habits, wondering why the life and excitement have gone out of your faith?

Without vision, intimacy with God is impossible. Jacob had to *see* God before he could *know* God! Many of us go to church Sunday after Sunday with no bigger dream than our next meal or our next paycheck. We can't see beyond the here and now. When we come into the house of God, when we return to divine order and our vision is restored, God gives us dreams for our children and their children for generations to come. He gives us a vision for our lives, our families, and our communities.

Jacob's vision at Bethel gave him spiritual empowerment. It caused him to realize that a direct path was open between him and God. There was nothing that he would go through where God was not with him, strengthening him and sustaining him. It awakened him to consciousness of his blessing. This empowerment released him in some ways from the "old" Jacob. That night at Bethel, Jacob the "deceiver" began to die and Israel the "prince of God" or "he who will rule as God" began to be born. It would be many years before God formally changed Jacob's name to "Israel" (see Gen. 32:28) but the qualities that would mature into that new man were born at Bethel.

Jacob's vision at Bethel was key to what God was going to do in Jacob's life and in the life of his family. Our own personal vision of God is just as important for the same reason. It births in us an awareness of the divine destiny that is ours even from our mother's womb. That awareness changes our understanding of who we are; it changes our "name," so to speak. It awakens in us the desire to leave behind our "Jacob" nature and take up our new "Israel" nature as the people of God. We begin to see ourselves as who we *really* are in God—children of the King of kings—rather than as the weak, impotent, and irrelevant people who the world tells us we are. Bethel is where we receive the vision of God for our individual lives, for our communal lives, and for the lives of generations yet unborn. Bethel is the place of vision.

What about you? How fresh is your vision? When was the last time you "saw" God? Is He real to you right now? If not, why don't you take a moment to talk to Him? Ask God to restore your vision, to renew that intimacy with Him, and help you move from where you *are* to where He wants you to be.

Open Your Ears and Hear

Jacob had a vision at Bethel in which He saw God. In his vision Jacob also *heard* the *voice* of God. Bethel, then, is also the place to hear God's voice. God spoke *directly* to Jacob. For us, this means that when we are in the house of God, when we are in divine order, we can hear the voice of God. Hearing God speak is not the exclusive privilege of the preacher or prophet. Just as He did with Jacob, God wants to speak to *each* of us directly and personally. The question is, *are we listening*? If we are out of order, our spiritual ears are clogged and it is hard for us to hear God. That's why so many of us often feel as though God is far away and He doesn't answer our prayers. It's not a question of whether or not God is speaking; He is. Our problem is that we cannot hear Him because our lives are out of order. Jacob's experience contains a lesson for us.

When God spoke to Jacob, He told him three things about Himself. First of all, God told Jacob who He was. "I am the Lord God of Abraham your father and the God of Isaac" (Gen. 28:13a). The message here is that God is *personal* and that He relates to us on a *personal* level. In effect, God was saying, "Jacob, I am the God of your father and your grandfather. Isn't it about time that I became *your* God, too?" Before Jacob could follow God, he had to be absolutely clear about who God was.

It is the same with us. The reason so many of us are out of order with God is because we don't really know who God is. We may know a lot *about* Him from our parents or others, but we don't really *know* Him for ourselves. If we did, we would stop caring what other people think about us. We would start trying to please God rather than trying to please people. When we hear the voice of God, He will set us straight as to who He is: God Almighty, King of kings and Lord of lords, who loves us and wants us to love Him and relate to Him on a *personal* level.

The second thing that God said to Jacob about Himself was what He would be doing. "The land on which you lie I will give to you and your descendants. Also your descendants shall be as the dust of the earth; you shall spread abroad to the west and the east, to the north and the south; and in you and in your seed all the families of the earth shall be blessed" (Gen. 28:13b-14). God told Jacob that He would be busy carrying out the promise He had made to Abraham and Isaac (and was now reaffirming to Jacob) of fruitfulness, prosperity, and purpose in bringing forth a holy nation through whom all of the earth would be blessed. Jacob himself would be directly involved in the fulfillment of that promise.

When God speaks to us, He will not only reveal who He is but also what He is doing around us. He wants us to be doing what He is doing. When we (or our churches) get out of order, we become confused about what God is saying and lose sight of what God is doing. With no clue of what God is doing, we follow our own ideas and plans and then wonder why God doesn't bless us.

The third thing God told Jacob was where He would be. "Behold, I am with you and will keep you wherever you go, and will bring you back to this land; for I will not leave you until I have done what I have spoken to you" (Gen. 28:15). God promised that He would be with Jacob all the time. This constant divine presence would be Jacob's confidence and guarantee that the full promise would be accomplished. Jacob could go out, even into a far country, confident that his God was with him and would bring him back to the land promised to him.

Thanks be to God! He will never leave us or forsake us! No matter how dry our wilderness or how seemingly hopeless our situation, our God is with us and, if we let Him, will lead us back to the promised land of His blessing. We must be willing to seek the voice of God.

When Jacob heard the voice of God, the vision of God changed his life. That voice released him from bondage to the other voices in his life—those self-centered voices that blocked his ability to understand what God was doing in his life. Only when God spoke to Jacob were his eyes opened. What a difference that voice made! If once we hear the voice of God, we will never forget it!

That voice is just what many Christians today are missing. They attend "worship," go through their "religious" motions, but never hear the voice of God. We desperately need to hear God's voice today. If God would speak to a lying, scheming scoundrel like Jacob and change his life, surely He will do the same for us. God wants to speak to the one caught up in adultery or pornography. He wants to speak to those who were physically or sexually abused as children. God wants to speak to the woman who was raped and who feels so ashamed that she has never spoken of it, even after ten or twenty years. He wants to speak to the junkie, the alcoholic, the one trapped in the dead-end life of the streets. God wants to speak to that single mom or dad working two or three jobs to support their children and who have no peace of mind or spirit. There is no area of our lives that God does not want to speak to. We must learn to open our ears and hear.

Open Your Hearts and Believe

When Jacob awoke from his dream, everything around him looked different. On the surface nothing had changed. *Jacob* was different. He had received a divine *visitation* that forever after cast his world in a different hue. Bethel was a place of *visitation*. "Then Jacob awoke from his sleep and said, 'Surely the Lord is in this place, and I did not know it.' And he was afraid and said, 'How awesome is this place! This is none other than the house of God, and this is the

25

gate of heaven!' " (Gen. 28:16-17) Jacob was almost overwhelmed by what had happened. God had visited him, leaving him awed, fearful, and humbled. For probably the first time in his life, Jacob was aware of the reality and presence of God in a very personal way.

One of the big problems we face today is that our churches are full of people who have never had a deeply personal experience with God for themselves. They may be saved and know a lot *about* God but He is not personally real and close to them on a regular, day-by-day basis. Many of these folks are what I call spiritual parasites. They live off of someone else's singing or someone else's testimony or someone else's experience. They live off of the preacher's sermon, or off of this conference or that conference. Only rarely does anything fresh and new happen for them *personally* in their Christian walk.

God desires a love relationship with each of us where He can visit us not only in church on Sunday morning, but also at home, at the workplace, at the grocery store, at school—anywhere. The key is our openness. We must be open to the vision and the voice of God if we are to receive the visitation of God.

It is very important that we understand that even though God seeks a relationship with us, the final decision is ours. We are responsible for doing our part. Any relationship takes time to develop. If you love someone, you desire to build a relationship with him or her. The only way to do that is to spend time with that person. It is the same way with our relationship with God. Simply going to church for two hours every Sunday won't cut it. It's a good start, perhaps, but it is not enough. Dusting off our Bible and bringing it to church once a week won't do either. Nor will praying at the altar once a week—if that's the only time we pray. If we want to *know* God, we must spend *time* with Him. If we want the visitation of God in our everyday lives, we must take the time to build our relationship with Him.

Many folks, even in the church, claim that they are too busy to spend time with God. They're busy with their jobs or with soccer or with Little League or with football. They're "busy" watching professional wrestling or sitcoms on TV. They're busy with everything

26

under the sun *except* God. If we're too busy to pray, we're too busy. If we're too busy to read and study God's Word, we're too busy. If we're too busy to spend time in God's house with God's people doing God's business, we're too busy. Too often our "busyness" puts us out of order with God. If we take time for God, however, God will take time for us. If we take time to talk to God, He will talk to us; if we take time to listen, we will hear His voice. If we take time to read God's Word, and seek His presence, He will respond to us and give us a visitation.

Bethel, then, is a house of visitation, a place where God visits us even in our pain and our brokenness. It is the place where God comes to us not *because* of who we are, but *in spite of* who we are—in spite of our sins, in spite of the abuses of our past, in spite of our rebellion. When God visits us in spite of ourselves, His great grace and mercy flood our souls and we become deeply aware of how unworthy we are. This sense of unworthiness does not humiliate us, but humbles us. That humility prepares our hearts—makes us ready—for the restoration that God's visitation brings. When God visits us, He is inviting us to be restored. God wants to come to us right where we are, not because we deserve it but because we need it. His visitation is not based on our performance but on His mercy and grace. He asks us to open our hearts and believe.

A Place of Remembrance

Jacob arrived at Bethel as a vagabond, a man on the run; he left Bethel as a visionary. God had appeared to him, spoken to him, and called him, and now Jacob had a different motivation and an entirely new perspective on life. Such a significant turning point could not go unacknowledged.

Then Jacob rose early in the morning, and took the stone that he had put at his head, set it up as a pillar, and poured oil on top of it. And he called the name of that place Bethel; but the name of that city had been Luz previously. Then Jacob made a vow, saying, "If God will be with me, and keep me in this way that I am going, and give me bread to eat and clothing to put on, so that I come back to my father's house in peace, then the Lord shall be my God. And this stone which I have set as a pillar shall be God's house, and of all that You give me I will surely give a tenth to You" (Genesis 28:18-22).

Jacob arrived at Bethel as a schemer and a man who lived by his wits; he left as a man who *walked with God.* What this says to us is that we should never give up hope no matter what we have done, no matter what mistakes we have made, no matter how low we have fallen or how sneaky we have been. As long as we have life, there is hope that God will meet us and turn our lives around. He stands ready and waiting; He waits for you and for me.

For Jacob, Bethel was a place of remembrance to which he could always point and say, "That's where God met me and changed my life." All of us need such a place of remembrance, a reminder that no matter who or what we used to be, God is making us into someone completely new. As unworthy as we are, God considers us worthy of His visitation. Bethel is the house of visitation where God meets us in our need and moves us from pain to power and from tragedy to triumph. Whenever the enemy brings to my mind the dark side of my past and all my sinful actions, I can simply look back to the day God met me and remember that who I was then is not who I am now or who I will be in the future. Praise God, He has changed me, and the best is yet to come!

Jacob left Bethel a changed man. Now he walked with God. There was still a very long road and many difficult years ahead, but he was on the track that would enable God to fulfill His promises. The Bethel experience transformed Jacob from a vagabond to a visionary. During the years ahead, God would change him from rogue to royalty, and Jacob would return to Bethel with a new name: Israel—"he who rules as God."

CHAPTER THREE

From Rogue to Royalty

At Bethel God began to put Jacob's life back in order, but there was still a lot of work to be done. Jacob faced a long road on his journey from rogue to royalty and it lay *ahead* of him, not behind him in the direction of home. Walking with God meant stepping forth boldly into unknown territory. God had promised Jacob, "Behold, I am with you and will keep you *wherever you go*, and will bring you *back* to this land" (Gen. 28:15a). Sometime in the future Jacob would return to the land that the Lord had promised to him and his descendants, but for now God's purpose lay elsewhere.

"So Jacob went on his journey and came to the land of the people of the East" (Gen. 29:1). This was not a "Sunday drive" in the country; it was a long trip. Leaving Bethel, Jacob struck out to the east-northeast and crossed the Jordan River. East of the Jordan he turned more to the north, made his way past the city of Damascus and eventually crossed the Euphrates River. Finally, several weeks and over 400 miles later, Jacob arrived at Haran in the region of Paddan-Aram, where his mother's family lived. At last, Jacob felt safe. Not only had God promised to be with him, but Jacob was also confident that not even Esau would pursue him that far!

Jacob had arrived at Bethel with little more than the staff in his hand (see Gen. 32:10). He left Bethel with much more than that, although it was invisible to human eyes. Before departing, Jacob had taken the rock he had used as a pillow and set it up as a memorial pillar. He had then poured oil on the rock, anointing it as "Beth-el," the "house of God." Bethel was a place of anointing. Although he may have been little aware of it at the time, *Jacob left Bethel with the anointing of God on his life.* This would become clear in the years just ahead as God caused Jacob to prosper in every way, even despite great obstacles.

At Bethel, God reaffirmed to Jacob the covenant promise He had given to Abraham and Isaac. *Jacob left Bethel with the affirmation of God in his heart.* This affirmation would stand to encourage and strengthen Jacob during the difficult days that lay before him. Jacob's years in Haran would be a proving ground where God would mold his character, shaping him into the man he needed to be to fulfill God's purpose.

During those years of preparation, Jacob would grow to maturity and learn the importance of being accountable for his actions. Although it was no more than a sprouting seed in his soul at the time, *Jacob left Bethel with accountability to God in his spirit.* Before long he would have ample opportunity to demonstrate both his character and his accountability as he dealt with his uncle Laban. Jacob's ultimate test would come years later when he had to face Esau, the brother he had wronged.

Meeting His Match

When Jacob arrived in Haran, he began looking for his mother's family. It didn't take long. One day he met his cousin Rachel, a shepherdess, as she brought her flock to water at a communal well. Overjoyed to see a relative at last, Jacob helped her water her flock, then kissed her, wept, and told her who he was. Rachel ran home and told her father, Laban, who rushed to meet Jacob and welcomed him warmly (see Gen. 29:1-13).

A month passed and Laban offered to pay Jacob to work for him. When asked what wages he wanted, Jacob replied, "I will serve you seven years for Rachel your younger daughter" (Gen.

29:18). Laban readily agreed. Whether it was "love at first sight" that day when he watered her sheep at the well, or a feeling that grew over time, by the end of that first month Jacob was in love with Rachel, who was "beautiful of form and appearance" (Gen. 29:17b). We've all heard the saying that "love is blind," and it must have been true in Jacob's case, otherwise he would have seen what was coming. Smitten as he was, Jacob was completely blindsided by his uncle Laban.

"So Jacob served seven years for Rachel, and they seemed only a few days to him because of the love he had for her" (Gen. 29:20). Then Jacob asked Laban to follow through with their agreement and give him Rachel as his wife. It's said "what goes around comes around," and "be sure, your sins will find you out." Jacob the deceiver was about to be "had" by a master. In Laban, Jacob had met his match in the deception department. Laban was, as we might say today, a real "piece of work."

Laban threw a big wedding party for Jacob, then brought his bride to him. It was customary in that culture and that part of the world (and still is) for brides to be completely veiled when presented to their husbands. Because of this and because it was night, Jacob did not actually "see" his new wife until the following morning. Imagine Jacob's shock when he rolled over and looked into the face, not of Rachel, but of Leah, Rachel's older sister!

It must have been quite a scene when Jacob stormed out of the tent and confronted his uncle. "What's the meaning of this? What have you done to me? I worked seven years to get Rachel as my wife! Why did you give me Leah?"

I can just imagine the smug look on Laban's face. "Oh, didn't you know? It's not customary in our country to marry the younger daughter before the firstborn." Laban had known this was coming for a long time. During Jacob's seven years of labor, had there been no suitors at all for Leah? Could not Laban have married her off to another eligible young man in the area? Maybe Laban was convinced that Leah for some reason had few prospects for marriage and he had better grab whatever opportunity came along. Otherwise, he might be saddled with a spinster daughter for the rest of his life. Worse still, if he couldn't marry off Rachel until he married off Leah, he might end up with *two* spinster daughters to support! Or perhaps he simply thought it was a great joke to play on his nephew. Even more likely was that he saw the prospect of getting seven more years of "free" labor from Jacob.

Laban tried to smooth Jacob's ruffled feathers. "I'll tell you what, nephew. Finish out the customary 'honeymoon' week with Leah, and then I'll let you marry Rachel. In return, you'll work for me another seven years."

Jacob knew he'd been had. He loved Rachel, and the only way to have her as his wife was to work another seven years for his scheming uncle. It must have been a bitter taste in Jacob's mouth to be on the receiving end for a change.

As the Dust of the Earth

Jacob's response to Laban's deception reveals that he was already becoming a different man from the one he had been at home. It would have been easy for Jacob to have justified finding a way to get out of serving Laban for the second seven years and yet still keep Rachel. He did not do this, however. The first seven years, when he had labored in order to win the woman he loved, had built some character into Jacob. He now had some appreciation for the fruit of hard work. His awareness of his responsibility to God had grown also. Jacob no longer saw life so much as "me against the world," but as God working in his life to bring about the divine purpose. So Jacob served his uncle faithfully and honestly for another seven years.

The anointing of God on Jacob's life became evident during these years, particularly in the growth of his family. God had promised Jacob that his descendants would be "as the dust of the earth" (see Gen. 28:14), and in short order Jacob was well on his way. Leah, the "unloved" (see Gen. 29:31), bore Jacob six sons: Reuben, Simeon, Levi, Judah, Issachar, and Zebulon. She also bore him a daughter, Dinah. Leah's handmaid, Zilpah, whom Leah gave to Jacob as a wife, bore him two sons: Gad and Asher. Rachel also gave her handmaid, Bilhah, to Jacob as a wife, and Bilhah also bore

Jacob two sons: Dan and Naphtali. Rachel herself was barren for many years, but finally the Lord answered her prayers and she conceived and gave birth to Joseph. Years later, during the journey back to Beersheba, Rachel also gave birth to Benjamin. These twelve sons of Jacob became the patriarchs—the fathers—of each of the twelve tribes of the nation of Israel. Fulfillment of God's promise to Abraham was underway!

Jacob's fruitfulness was not limited to his family. He also prospered in the accumulation of wealth, particularly in abundance of sheep and goats. These he acquired through honest effort and the providence of God, in spite of Laban's efforts to trick and cheat him.

One day shortly after Joseph was born, Jacob told Laban he wanted to take his family and return to his own country (see Gen. 30:25-26). Nowhere here does the Scripture indicate that *God* had spoken to Jacob about returning home. The time wasn't right. God still had plans for Jacob in Haran. Laban prevailed upon Jacob to stay and keep tending the flocks, acknowledging that he himself had prospered because of Jacob's hard work. Jacob agreed, on the condition that he could take as his wages all the speckled and spotted sheep and goats from Laban's flocks to build flocks of his own. Laban readily agreed (where have we heard *that* before!).

Behind Jacob's back, Laban, that sly devil, immediately removed all the speckled and spotted animals from his flocks, put them in the care of his sons, and sent them a three-day's journey away (see Gen. 30:35-36). I'm sure Laban thought he had pulled another fast one on his nephew. Crafty though he was, Laban hadn't reckoned on the God of Abraham, Isaac, and Jacob!

Genesis 30:37-43 relates how during the six *additional* years that Jacob kept Laban's livestock, Jacob's own stock grew large while his uncle's flocks bore speckled and spotted animals. In addition, the stronger animals bore speckled and spotted offspring while the weaker ones did not. So, Jacob's flocks not only grew larger in numbers than Laban's, but Jacob's animals were also physically stronger and healthier than Laban's. The scriptural account suggests that Jacob employed some craftiness of his own, but when we read between the lines we can see that God was prospering Jacob at Laban's expense.

Laban's cunning was no match for the anointing of God that rested on Jacob's life. Jacob, the "recovering heel-catcher," was a prince of God in the making, and God was determined to prosper him, bless him, and fulfill His covenant promise through him. By the standards of that day Jacob became quite wealthy. He was "exceedingly prosperous, and had large flocks, female and male servants, and camels and donkeys" (Gen. 30:43). This was none of Jacob's doing; it was the anointing of God.

Where's the Anointing?

When Jacob left Bethel, he had not been anointed with physical oil; his anointing was spiritual. In fact, throughout Scripture, oil is used as a symbol of the Spirit of God. God's Spirit anointed Jacob at Bethel, and he carried that anointing with him wherever he went. This anointing was a spiritual connection between Jacob and God that broke the yoke that bound Jacob to his old life. The presence of God was so rich at Bethel that the anointing began to totally reshape Jacob's life, and he was never again the same. He began to move from selfishness to servanthood, from trust in himself to trust in God, and from being a deceiver to being a prince of God. Such a transformation can happen only under the presence of God's anointing.

One of the reasons God's house is out of order today is because we have stepped out from under the anointing. When we lose intimacy with God, we lose sight of His anointing. We wander off the straight and narrow path of life into the broad way which leads to destruction (see Mt. 7:13-14). While God is at work in one place, we are busy someplace else, wondering why we aren't doing any good. Godly purpose, divine direction, spiritual power, and genuine effectiveness are possible only under the anointing. Another way to say this is that it is only when we *see* God (vision), *hear* God (voice), and *walk* in the presence of God in faith and obedience (visitation), that we can realize our spiritual destiny and fulfill God's purpose. Walking in God's presence means walking in His anointing.

The house of God should be an anointed house. The people of God should be anointed people. Every usher should be anointed before standing at any door. Every choir member should be anointed before singing a note. Every preacher should be anointed before speaking a word. Every person sitting in the pew should be anointed before serving in any ministry. I'm not talking about physical anointing with oil; I'm talking about Holy Spirit anointing. When we are out of order—out from under God's anointing—we wander around in the yoke of sin and blindness, being confused, weak, and powerless. We need to cry out, "Restore us, Lord! Bring us back under Your anointing! Touch us, O God! We want to sit in an anointed place, eat in an anointed place, worship with anointed people!" Why? *The anointing breaks the yoke*. It sets us free to be God's people going about God's business in God's way.

God won't force us to walk in the anointing. That choice is up to us, and what we choose will make all the difference in what happens next. None of us should ever leave the house without saying, "Anoint me, Lord. Anoint my mind so that I think right; anoint my mouth so that I speak right." The Lord's anointing will change our lives and empower our churches. If we are going to restore the house of God, we must repent and return to the anointing of God.

The anointing is only the beginning. Many of us are ready to stop there, but the anointing is not a stopping place; it is a *starting* place. *The anointing prepares us for the glory of God*. It makes us "smell good" to God. The anointing covers all our sins and our weaknesses and allows us to come into the presence of God, where we experience the glory of God. When the glory of God comes, miracles happen. I don't know about you, but I don't want just the anointing, I want the glory of God! Restore Your house, O Lord! Restore Your anointing! Bring down Your glory!

Homeward Bound

Twenty years had passed since Jacob had left Beersheba and fled to Haran. I wonder how often during that time he longed to see his home and his parents, or how many times he regretted the way he had treated his brother. As the years passed, how often did Jacob remember the words of affirmation he had received from the Lord at Bethel, and wonder when they would come to pass?

> ..."*I am the Lord God of Abraham your father and the God of Isaac; the land on which you lie I will give to you and your descendants. Also your descendants shall be as the dust of the earth; you shall spread abroad to the west and the east, to the north and the south; and in you and in your seed all the families of the earth shall be blessed. Behold, I am with you and will keep you wherever you go, and will bring you back to this land; for I will not leave you until I have done what I have spoken to you*" (Genesis 28:13-15).

Twenty years in one place is a long time, particularly in a nomadic culture, and as both Jacob's family and prosperity grew, he began to wear out his welcome in his uncle's house. Laban's sons began to grumble about their cousin and accused Jacob of cheating their father in order to enrich himself. Laban must have felt the same way because his attitude toward Jacob changed. "And Jacob saw the countenance of Laban, and indeed it was not favorable toward him as before" (Gen. 31:2). Their relationship was quickly turning sour.

It was just at this juncture that God spoke to Jacob. By human reckoning, God sometimes seems slow to act, but in reality He is right on time—rarely early and *never* late. The Lord gave Jacob affirmation right when he needed it the most. "Return to the land of your fathers and to your family, and I will be with you" (Gen. 31:3). God's time had come.

Calling Rachel and Leah to him, Jacob explained to them what God had said to him, revealing in the process both his understanding of the relationship between Laban and himself, and his awareness of God's protective presence with him.

> ..."*I see your father's countenance, that it is not favorable toward me as before; but the God of my father has been with me. And you know that with all my might I have served your father. Yet your father has deceived me and changed my wages ten*

*times, but God did not allow him to hurt me. If he said thus:
'The speckled shall be your wages,' then all the flocks bore speckled. And if he said thus: 'The streaked shall be your wages,' then
all the flocks bore streaked. So God has taken away the livestock
of your father and given them to me"* (Genesis 31:5-9).

Do you see how much Jacob had changed and matured over
the years? Now he saw the hand of God (the anointing) on everything in his life, and he credited God for all his success and prosperity. What's even more important is that everything Jacob had
now he had acquired through honest, hard work rather than
through deceit. Through it all God, in His divine providence, had
repeatedly affirmed Jacob and blessed him.

Jacob then told Rachel and Leah of the strongest affirmation
of all: the Word of the Lord.

*"Then the Angel of God spoke to me in a dream, saying, 'Jacob.'
And I said, 'Here I am.' And He said, 'Lift your eyes now and
see, all the rams which leap on the flocks are streaked, speckled,
and gray-spotted; for I have seen all that Laban is doing to you.
I am the God of Bethel, where you anointed the pillar and where
you made a vow to Me. Now arise, get out of this land, and
return to the land of your family'"* (Genesis 31:11-13).

Rachel and Leah needed little persuading; they were as ready
to leave as Jacob was. Because of the strained relationship with
Laban, Jacob and his family decided to depart quickly without letting him know they were leaving. Laban was away shearing his
sheep. Three days passed before he learned that Jacob was gone.

Affirmative Action

For Jacob, Bethel was a place of affirmation in two ways.
First, it was the place where God affirmed to him the
covenant promise to make of him a great nation. At the
same time, the Lord promised to be with Jacob, to protect and
prosper him, and to bring him back to his homeland. Second,
Bethel was where Jacob made an affirmation, or vow to God, saying that if God would indeed do all of those things, then Jacob

would serve God and follow Him. Jacob was not trying to "make a deal" with God; he acknowledged God's promise and committed himself to God's care. It was the major turning point of his life.

God is still in the affirming business today, but many of us are too out of order to listen. He wants to affirm and encourage us with the promise of His presence and His blessings. God longs to draw us to His side, love us, and fellowship with us. When we allow our house to get out of order, we lose sight of these things. The enemy and the "spirit of religion" come in and steal away our awareness of our special place in God's affection as His beloved children. Once we lose that sense of divine affirmation, we become prone to fear, insecurity, confusion, deception, depression, and desperation.

The house of God should be a house of affirmation where we hear the Lord's affirming words to us and where we make our vows to Him in faith. Most of us are quite ready to receive from God, but unwilling to make a vow to Him. A vow is a promise and that involves commitment. We live in a society that is afraid of commitment. That's why it's so hard to pin down politicians on where they stand on issues. That's why so many young couples today choose to live together instead of getting married. That's why so many people balk at taking a definite stand on anything; they don't want to offend anyone or be thought of as "intolerant."

Many church people have been deceived into thinking that they can have *belief* without conviction, *faith* without commitment, and *religion* without responsibility. Well, I've got news for you. *Faith* that requires nothing, demands nothing, and costs us nothing *is* nothing! James said that "faith without works is dead" (Jas. 2:20b). Passive faith that does not go beyond mere words is nothing more than pious-sounding hot air. It is not true faith. True faith is active, not passive. Genuine faith is our active response to the affirming actions of God toward us.

I find it hard to understand why we have such a problem making a commitment to God. After all, look at what He has *already done* for us! Think about how good God has been to you! Think about the food on your table, the clothes on your back, and the money in your pocket because the Lord answered your prayer for that job you needed so badly. Think about all that Christ delivered you out of. Think about that liquor you used to drink, or that reefer you used to smoke, or those needles you used to put in your arm. Think about that abusive, dead-end relationship He freed you from. Paul said that "while we were still sinners, Christ died for us" (Rom. 5:8b). No matter who we are or what we've done, Jesus has *already* died for us! When He gets hold of our lives, He changes our way of walking, our way of talking, our way of thinking—He changes everything about us! He lifts us out of the gutter, cleans us up, and makes us royal children of the King of kings! He gives us victory after the world has knocked us down time after time after time! After all Christ has done for us, how can we *not* commit our lives to Him?

If God could take an old rogue like Jacob and turn him around, change him, and raise up a great nation through him, just think what He can do with us if we let Him! What greater affirmation could Jacob have received than when God said, "Jacob, it doesn't matter who you were or what you've done; what matters is who I make you to be. Follow Me and a great nation will come from your loins, a nation through whom I will bless all the peoples of the earth." God wants to affirm us the same way. It doesn't matter who we are or what we've done. *What matters is who we become in Him!* That makes all the difference in the world.

Day of Reckoning

As soon as Laban heard that Jacob and his family had fled, he gathered his brethren and set out in hot pursuit (see Gen. 31:23). He caught up with Jacob and his band a week later in the mountains of Gilead. At that point, things might have gone badly for Jacob had God not warned Laban in a dream to be very careful how he spoke and acted toward Jacob (see Gen. 31:24). Perhaps Laban's anger and jealousy toward Jacob had reached a fever pitch, or perhaps he didn't like the thought of losing Jacob's labor and services. Whatever Laban's motivation, only the Lord's intervention prevented him from harming Jacob (see Gen. 31:29).

Laban claimed that he was looking for his "household gods," idols which had been stolen from his house. Rachel had taken them, but Jacob did not know about it. After Laban searched Jacob's tents and all their belongings and found nothing (Rachel had hidden them well), Jacob challenged his uncle. In hot indignation Jacob asserted his innocence and called God as a witness to his years of faithful, honest service for Laban.

> *"These twenty years I have been with you; your ewes and your female goats have not miscarried their young, and I have not eaten the rams of your flock. That which was torn by beasts I did not bring to you; I bore the loss of it. You required it from my hand, whether stolen by day or stolen by night. There I was! In the day the drought consumed me, and the frost by night, and my sleep departed from my eyes. Thus I have been in your house twenty years; I served you fourteen years for your two daughters, and six years for your flock, and you have changed my wages ten times. Unless the God of my father, the God of Abraham and the Fear of Isaac, had been with me, surely now you would have sent me away empty-handed. God has seen my affliction and the labor of my hands, and rebuked you last night"* (Genesis 31:38-42).

Jacob's spirited defense helped clear the air and afterward, he and Laban reconciled. They made a covenant, each pledging never to go against the other for harm. The next day Laban returned to his home (see Gen. 31:43-55).

This final confrontation between Jacob and Laban reveals another aspect of Jacob's Bethel experience—accountability. Jacob's years in Haran had taught him the importance of being accountable for his actions. Laban's pursuit forced Jacob into the position of being accountable to his uncle. Sometimes it hurts when we have to be accountable to someone who has less integrity than we do. I'm sure it hurt Jacob, too. That's why he responded in anger to Laban's demands. This experience of accountability did two things for Jacob. First, it made clear to everyone how God had changed his character and second, it helped prepare Jacob for the even greater accountability he would soon face.

God expects His people to be accountable. He holds us accountable for our words and our actions, our thoughts and our attitudes. The apostle Paul wrote, "Moreover it is required in stewards that one be found faithful" (1 Cor. 4:2). As the people of God, we are His stewards and faithfulness involves accountability. If our spiritual house is going to be in order, we must be accountable to God in all things. *Bethel is a place of accountability.*

Sleepless Night

As Jacob and his company continued their journey, he knew that his greatest test lay just ahead. He had to face Esau. After sending messengers to Esau to announce his arrival, Jacob was distressed to hear upon their return that Esau was coming to meet *him* with 400 men. Despite all the evidence of God's care and providence over the past 20 years, Jacob succumbed to a very human fear. *Surely, Esau can't have been waiting all this time just to kill me!* Nevertheless, Jacob took wise precautions. He divided his family and belongings into two groups and sent each ahead separately, so that if Esau attacked one group, the other might survive. Jacob also sent servants ahead with a large number of animals from his flocks as a generous gift to his brother.

After he had done everything humanly possible to prepare for his meeting with Esau, Jacob humbled himself in prayer before his God, reminding God of His promises and praying for His protection. Jacob truly was a changed man.

... "O God of my father Abraham and God of my father Isaac, the Lord who said to me, 'Return to your country and to your family, and I will deal well with you': I am not worthy of the least of all the mercies and of all the truth which You have shown Your servant; for I crossed over this Jordan with my staff, and now I have become two companies. Deliver me, I pray, from

the hand of my brother, from the hand of Esau; for I fear him, lest he come and attack me and the mother with the children. For You said, 'I will surely treat you well, and make your descendants as the sand of the sea, which cannot be numbered for multitude' " (Genesis 32:9-12).

All of Jacob's family, servants, and belongings were taken across the brook called Jabbok, leaving him alone on the other side. The stage was now set for the event for which God had been preparing Jacob for 20 years.

Then Jacob was left alone; and a Man wrestled with him until the breaking of day. Now when He saw that He did not prevail against him, He touched the socket of his hip; and the socket of Jacob's hip was out of joint as He wrestled with him. And He said, "Let Me go, for the day breaks." But he said, "I will not let You go unless You bless me!" So He said to him, "What is your name?" He said, "Jacob." And He said, "Your name shall no longer be called Jacob, but Israel; for you have struggled with God and with men, and have prevailed." Then Jacob asked, saying, "Tell me Your name, I pray." And He said, "Why is it that you ask about My name?" And He blessed him there. So Jacob called the name of the place Peniel: "For I have seen God face to face, and my life is preserved" (Genesis 32:24-30).

See how thoroughly Jacob had been changed by his Bethel experience! Jacob had grown so to love, even to crave, the anointing of God (the blessing) that he couldn't stand to live without it. He held on and prevailed for the blessing, even with a dislocated hip. That's hunger! That's perseverance! When was the last time *you* were that hungry and persistent for the anointing and blessing of God?

Here too Jacob faced his ultimate accountability, even greater than that which he owed to Esau. The Man with whom Jacob wrestled asked him, "What is your name?" When Jacob answered, he did much more than simply identify himself. By acknowledging his name as "Jacob," he also acknowledged everything that went along with that name. When Jacob said, "My name is Jacob," he was also saying, "My name is 'Heel-catcher'; my name is 'Deceiver'; my name is 'Supplanter'; my name is 'Liar'; my name is 'Con man'; my name is 'Slickster'; my name is 'Trickster.' " Jacob was accountable to God for who he was and who he had been.

When Jacob acknowledged his accountability for who he was, God released him from it, freeing him to become who he *would be* by the grace of God. This opened the way for God's greatest affirmation of all: "Your name shall no longer be called Jacob, but Israel; for you have struggled with God and with men, and have prevailed" (Gen. 32:28). God changed Jacob's name to reflect his changed character. Jacob the "deceiver" became Israel, the "prince of God," or "he who rules as God." Beginning at Bethel, God had shaped, grown, and matured Jacob over the years to transform him into a man suitable to be the father of a holy nation.

Jacob went on from there with a limp to remind him of his struggle, his divine encounter, his change of character, and his victory. He had wrestled with himself as much as with the presence of God, and had prevailed. God answered his prayers. Esau welcomed Jacob with joy and good favor. The brothers were reconciled, and it was all because God had met Jacob at Bethel years before and changed him forever.

Just as Jacob was accountable to God for himself, so are we. Once we acknowledge our accountability, God releases us from it. This is called confession. It is saying, "God, I know I was wrong. I know there is more to life than this. From now on, I will be accountable to you. I give myself to you. Take who I was and make me into who you want me to be."

Bethel was an intensely personal experience for Jacob; it was his *unique* and *personal* encounter with the living God. The Lord relates to every person on a one-to-one basis. That's the way He operates. The house of God cannot be restored on a *corporate* level until the people of God are restored on a *personal* level. Each one of us must "go to Bethel" for ourselves. God has no grandchildren. He deals with each of us individually. *Everybody has a "Bethel"!*

CHAPTER FOUR

Everybody Has a Bethel

There's an old Negro spiritual that says, "You can run, but you can't hide." Jacob ran, and ended up running right into God. The Lord had plans for Jacob, and the first step in those plans was to bring Jacob into a personal relationship with Himself. I seriously doubt that a relationship with God was on Jacob's mind when he fled his home and family, but unknown to him, God was directing his steps. The more Jacob ran, the closer he came to Bethel. When he got there, God was waiting for him.

Like Jacob, millions of people today are on the run. They're so busy making a living that they don't have time to *live*. Many have no ties of any kind to the Church and don't want any, while many others who were raised with religious training have left the Church for one reason or another. Whatever their status, they are all running from God as fast as they can, not knowing that He is already waiting up ahead. For some, running is the only way they will ever find what they need. While they may be fleeing "religion," they're about to run right into a relationship with Almighty God.

It's not just people in the "world" who are running, however. One of the reasons the house of God needs to be restored today is because it is filled with runners. We can see them on any given

Sunday in any church in the land. They may be sitting motionless in the pews, but their hearts are rushing and their minds racing as they try desperately to hide from God. It's sad to say, but much of the time the "runners" *inside* the Church do not meet God as easily and quickly as some of the "runners" *outside* the Church. Individuals and churches that are out of divine order have lost touch with the *personal* element of faith, often substituting impersonal rites, rituals, and regulations for a genuine experience with God. If we want to restore the house of God, we must recover this personal dynamic.

The God of the Bible is a *personal* God; He is a God of *relationship*. Throughout the Scriptures we see the Lord meeting individual people in a real and uniquely personal love relationship. In fact, the *only* way to know God is through a *personal encounter* that *He* initiates!

Everybody needs to "go to Bethel." "Bethel" is where we meet God personally and individually—that particular time, place, or circumstance where God steps into our lives and becomes real to us. Bethel is where we come face-to-face with the grace, mercy, and love of God. Bethel is where God changes us forever. *Everybody has a Bethel!*

God *always* works with individuals at the personal level. If you have trouble believing that God really wants to "get personal" with you, consider these accounts of real people who met God at their own personal "Bethel." Some are Bible characters, and some are people from later church history. I have even included my own story. Take it from me, *everybody has a Bethel.* All of these are stories of *ordinary people*, weak and flawed people who ran into God and were changed forever by their encounter.

Fire in the Bush

Moses had it all. Born a Hebrew slave in Egypt, he was plucked from the bulrushes and raised in pharaoh's own household. Educated and groomed as a royal prince, Moses' future looked bright. One day, however, in a single moment of uncontrolled anger, it all seemed to crumble away; and

Moses, prince of pharaoh, found himself a fugitive in a foreign land with Egyptian blood on his hands. An outcast and a murderer, Moses settled in Midian, married a Midianite woman, and became a shepherd. It took 40 years in the halls of pharaoh and 40 years in the hills of Midian before Moses was ready to run into God. Moses' "Bethel" was a burning bush on the side of Mount Horeb.

> *So when the Lord saw that he turned aside to look, God called to him from the midst of the bush and said, "Moses, Moses!" And he said, "Here I am."...Moreover He said, "I am the God of your father; the God of Abraham, the God of Isaac, and the God of Jacob." And Moses hid his face, for he was afraid to look upon God. And the Lord said: "I have surely seen the oppression of My people who are in Egypt, and have heard their cry because of their taskmasters, for I know their sorrows. So I have come down to deliver them out of the hand of the Egyptians....Come now, therefore, and I will send you to Pharaoh that you may bring My people, the children of Israel, out of Egypt"* (Exodus 3:4,6-8a,10).

God met Moses *personally* and revealed Himself in a unique way. No other "burning bush" event is recorded in Scripture. The Lord extended to Moses a *personal* call to be involved in His purpose of delivering the Hebrews from Egypt, and promised His *personal* presence. Moses left Horeb a changed man who walked with God for 40 more years. God used him to free Israel from Egyptian slavery and to lead and prepare them to enter the land God had promised to their fathers. Before any of this could happen though, Moses had to come to know God through a *personal* encounter. Moses had to "go to Bethel."

Smoke in the Temple

The death of a king, particularly a good king, was always a difficult time for the Israelites. Such a death may have played a part in prompting the life-changing vision that came to Isaiah one day. "In the year that King Uzziah died, I saw the Lord sitting on a throne, high and lifted up, and the train of His robe filled the temple" (Is. 6:1). Surrounding the Lord on His throne were seraphim, angels who praised God continually and hastened to do His bidding. The cries of "Holy, holy, holy is the Lord of hosts," were loud enough to shake the very door posts, and the temple was filled with smoke.

Such a vision of the glory, holiness, and majesty of God had a profound effect upon Isaiah. Like Jacob, Isaiah recognized his own sinfulness and unworthiness. "So I said: 'Woe is me, for I am undone! Because I am a man of unclean lips, and I dwell in the midst of a people of unclean lips; for my eyes have seen the King, the Lord of hosts' " (Is. 6:5).

Upon this confession, one of the seraphim flew to Isaiah and symbolically cleansed his sin by touching his lips with a live coal from the altar. It was then that Isaiah heard the call. "Also I heard the voice of the Lord, saying: 'Whom shall I send, and who will go for Us?' Then I said, 'Here am I! Send me.' And He said, 'Go...' " (Is. 6:8-9a).

Isaiah's life changed forever the day he had his personal encounter with God. When confronted with the revelation of God in His glory, Isaiah was moved to confess and repent of his sins. After God's revelation came God's *invitation* to Isaiah to join himself to the holy and divine purpose of the Lord. First came the personal encounter, then came the personal call. Isaiah answered that call and became one of the greatest of the Old Testament prophets. Whenever God initiates a personal encounter *with* us, He *always* calls for a personal response *from* us.

Light in the Sky (Paul)

For Saul (later Paul) of Tarsus, "Bethel" came somewhere on the road between Jerusalem and Damascus. A fervent Pharisee trying desperately to serve God, Saul was on a self-appointed mission to Damascus to ferret out "blasphemous" Jews who were followers of the dead heretic, Jesus of Nazareth. God arrested him dead in his tracks.

As he journeyed he came near Damascus, and suddenly a light shone around him from heaven. Then he fell to the ground, and heard a voice saying to him, "Saul, Saul, why are you persecuting Me?" And he said, "Who are You, Lord?" Then the Lord said, "I am Jesus, whom you are persecuting. It is hard for you to kick against the goads." So he, trembling and astonished, said, "Lord, what do You want me to do?" Then the Lord said to him, "Arise and go into the city, and you will be told what you must do" (Acts 9:3-6).

Blinded and humbled, Saul was led into Damascus. Three days later, his sight was restored during the visit of a Christian believer named Ananias, who said to Saul, "The God of our fathers has chosen you that you should know His will, and see the Just One, and hear the voice of His mouth. For you will be His witness to all men of what you have seen and heard" (Acts 22:14-15).

As a devout Pharisee, Saul had been running from God and didn't even know it. God met him on the run, knocked him down, turned him around, and set his life in a totally new direction. Paul's ministry to the Gentiles resulted in the gospel of Christ being spread to every corner of the "civilized" world by the end of the first century. Paul's "Bethel" was real, unique, and *personal*. When once we meet the Lord in our own personal "Bethel," we will never again be the same.

The Light of Full Certainty

Bethel represents the moment in time when a person meets God in a life-changing encounter, but the *road* to Bethel is not always quick, the arrival not always sudden. Such was the case with Augustine (354-430). Born in Carthage, in northern Africa, and raised in the teachings of Christ by his Christian mother, Monica, Augustine nevertheless did not embrace the faith in his youth. He opted instead to immerse himself in the secular education and philosophies of his day and to pursue a life of hedonistic and sexual pleasure. For many years he kept a mistress.

Through his early adult years, Augustine grew increasingly disillusioned and restless with the emptiness of his life and gradually began to reexamine the Christian teachings of his youth. The more he learned about Christ and the gospel, however, the more distressed he became. A fierce struggle raged in his spirit between the claims of the gospel and the temptations of the world. The conflict nearly tore him apart.

Finally, one day when Augustine, in a greatly agitated state of mind, was walking in the garden of his home, God's moment came. Augustine later wrote:

> I was...weeping in the most bitter contrition of my heart, when suddenly I heard the voice of a boy or a girl I know not which—coming from the neighboring house, chanting over and over again, "Pick it up, read it; pick it up, read it." Immediately I ceased weeping and began most earnestly to think whether it was usual for children in some kind of game to sing such a song, but I could not remember ever having heard the like. So, damming the torrent of my tears, I got to my feet, for I could not but think that this was a divine command to open the Bible and read the first passage I should light upon....
>
> I snatched it up, opened it, and in silence read the paragraph on which my eyes first fell: "Not in rioting and drunkenness, not in chambering and wantonness, not in strife and envying, but put on the Lord Jesus Christ, and make no provision for the flesh to fulfill the lusts thereof." [Rom. 13:13-14] I wanted to read no further, nor did I need to. For instantly, as the sentence ended, there was infused in my heart something like the light of full certainty and all the gloom of doubt vanished away.[1]

Augustine's "Bethel" was a garden in Milan, Italy in 386. There God spoke through His Word directly to Augustine's heart, settled his conflict, and for the next 44 years Augustine followed the Lord faithfully as a pastor, theologian, and teacher, eventually becoming bishop of Hippo. Regarded as one of the greatest theologians and intellects in the history of the Church, Augustine's influence is still felt throughout the Church today.

Justified by Faith

Upon completion of his bachelor's and master's degrees from the University of Erfurt, Germany, in 1505, Martin Luther (1483-1546) began studying for a law degree. A close brush with death later that same year turned his life in a different direction. He entered an Augustinian monastery in Erfurt, where he quickly rose in prominence and influence. Ordained a priest in 1507, Luther was sent to Wittenberg in 1508 to continue his studies. In 1511 he received his doctorate in theology and a permanent appointment as a professor of Bible at the University of Wittenberg.

The more this brilliant monk studied the Scriptures, particularly the writings of the apostle Paul, the more convinced he became that the standard teaching of the Catholic church concerning salvation was wrong. The church taught that people were responsible, at least in part, for earning their own righteousness before a wrathful God. Luther came to the understanding that justification (salvation) was by faith alone, made possible by the atoning death of Jesus Christ on the cross.

Luther's road to "Bethel" was a long and gradual one. As his dawning awareness grew of the role of faith in the process of salvation, he struggled for years to understand what Paul meant in Romans when he wrote, "For in it the righteousness of God is revealed from faith to faith; as it is written, 'The just shall live by faith' " (Rom. 1:17). Finally, one day in the year 1519, the revelation came in a burst of divine insight. Luther later wrote:

> I began to understand that this verse means that the justice of God is revealed through the Gospel, but it is a passive justice, i.e. that by which the merciful God justifies us by faith, as it is written: "The just person lives by faith." All at once I felt that I had been born again and entered into paradise itself through open gates. Immediately I

saw the whole of Scripture in a different light....I exalted this sweetest word of mine, "the justice of God," with as much love as before I had hated it with hate. This phrase of Paul was for me the very gate of paradise.[2]

As with Augustine centuries before, God spoke through His Word and His Spirit directly and personally into Martin Luther's heart and mind, resolved his conflict, removed his fear, and gave him the assurance that he was justified by faith alone. In the strength and confidence of this revelation, Luther became one of God's mighty instruments in reforming the Church and restoring to the forefront the doctrine—buried for centuries under tradition, distortion, and error—that people are made right with God not through their own efforts, but, by the grace of God, through faith in Christ *alone*.

In the Midst of the Tempest (John Newton)

By the age of 22, John Newton had already experienced more of life than most people three times his age. At sea since the age of 11, he had sailed the Atlantic numerous times, been pressed into service aboard a British warship, deserted, was recaptured, flogged, and disgraced, then traded to the crew of a slave ship. For a time he even lived as a slave to an African slave trader, and had finally risen to captain his own slave ship. Having long since abandoned the early religious instruction he had received from his mother, Newton had fallen into a life of drunkenness and moral depravity. He was the lowest of the low. John Newton was running from God, but God was ready to intercept him.

John Newton's "Bethel" came on the deck of his ship during a severe storm that threatened to founder the vessel. Sometime earlier, the seeds for his spiritual birth had been sown after he read a classic spiritual treatise, *The Imitation of Christ* by Thomas à Kempis. The night of May 10, 1748 was the time of Newton's "great deliverance." When the storm was at its height and it seemed all but certain that the ship would be lost, Newton cried out, "Lord, have mercy upon us!" The ship weathered the storm. In his cabin later on, Newton reflected on what had happened and realized that God had spoken to him through the storm and was working His grace in his life.[3]

Newton quit the slave trade shortly thereafter and by 1755 had left the sea altogether. He eventually entered the ministry as an Anglican priest and served faithfully as a pastor for the rest of his life. Among his friends were the great evangelist George Whitefield and John Wesley, the founder of Methodism. John Newton was also a hymn writer. The testimony of his personal, life-changing encounter with God is immortalized forever in the words of his most famous hymn, one of the most popular hymns in the Church:

> Amazing grace! How sweet the sound
> That saved a wretch like me.
> I once was lost, but now am found,
> Was blind, but now I see.

My Heart Strangely Warmed

In January 1736, John Wesley set sail from England for the Georgia colony in British North America with the mission and purpose of converting the Indians to Christianity. An intense and sober man, Wesley had long practiced great discipline in spiritual and religious exercises such as prayer, Bible study, and a strict lifestyle. He saw these things as the means to pleasing God, yet peace of mind and the assurance of God's favor continually eluded him.

During a severe storm at sea, Wesley was impressed by the calm faith of a group of Moravians who exhibited no fear of the tempest while the English passengers (including Wesley) were terrified. Their steady assurance in the face of possible death served to deepen Wesley's own uncertainty of where he stood with God.

Wesley's mission to Georgia and the Indians was a failure; he stayed less than two years. During this time his spiritual doubt and despair continued to grow. At one point on the return trip to England, he wrote in his journal, "I went to America, to convert the

Indians; but oh! who shall convert me?...I have a sin of fear, that when I've spun my last thread, I shall perish on the shore."[4]

Back in England, Wesley continued to struggle in his spirit even as he preached at every opportunity. Finally, on Wednesday, May 24, 1738, God's moment for John Wesley arrived. It was time for his "Bethel." Wesley described the event in his journal.

> In the evening I went very unwillingly to a society in Aldersgate Street, where one was reading Luther's preface to the Epistle to the Romans. About a quarter before nine, while he was describing the change which God works in the heart through faith in Christ, I felt my heart strangely warmed. I felt I did trust in Christ, Christ alone, for salvation; and an assurance was given me that He had taken away my sins, even mine, and saved me from the law of sin and death.[5]

This was a *personal* transaction between John Wesley and his Lord. God had forgiven *his* sins and had saved *him* from death. The peace and assurance that Wesley sought and which never came through his own efforts at being "religious" were suddenly his by the grace and mercy of God. John Wesley moved beyond his personal "Bethel," and God used him as a powerful force for revival and spiritual awakening in both England and America for the rest of the eighteenth century.

Richard Allen

One day in the year 1777 a group of slaves gathered in a clearing in the Delaware woods to hear a former slave owner-turned-itinerant-Methodist preacher proclaim the gospel. Among them was a 17-year-old field hand named Richard. Recently, Richard's world had been ripped apart when his mother and three siblings had been "sold down the river" by their financially strapped owner. Richard never saw them again. Perhaps it was turmoil in his spirit that drew Richard to the clearing that day. He was looking for an anchor in his life. Through the preaching of the aptly named Freeborn Garretson, Richard found that anchor.

Richard's "Bethel" was that clearing in the woods where God met him and opened his heart and mind to understand the truth of the gospel. The young slave gave his life to Christ that day, taking comfort in the assurance that, although he had been cut off from his family, he would never be cut off from God's love. Soon after, Richard began feeling a strong desire to preach. He wrote later in his autobiography, "I was constrained to go from house to house, exhorting my old companions and telling to all around what a dear Savior I had found."[6] He was instrumental in bringing about the conversion of his master, who later allowed Richard to hire himself out in order to earn money to buy his freedom. By the time he was 23, Richard was a free man. As an indicator of his new status, he adopted a surname and became Richard Allen, "free man of color."

Richard's burning desire was to preach the gospel. He obtained a Methodist "exhorter's license" and traveled extensively from state to state. Over the next decade or so, he developed a reputation as a powerful and effective preacher. He felt a particular burden for working to better the education and overall status of his people, both free and slave. One way he sought to do this was to establish a separate meeting and worship place for black Methodists in Philadelphia, who were suffering discrimination from whites in the racially mixed Methodist congregations. His efforts led eventually to the founding in 1816 of the African Methodist Episcopal (AME) church, the first completely independent black denomination in the country. Richard served as the group's first bishop until his death in 1831. At the time of his death, Richard Allen was a successful pastor and bishop, and a prosperous businessman in Philadelphia. He was responsible for helping to establish at least 11 black schools in the city as well as aid societies to assist black people in the city with both spiritual and material needs.

When Richard Allen went to "Bethel," God took a slave and raised him up to be a man of devotion, compassion, and influence in the kingdom of God.

Frank Reid

I have a long family history with the church. Ministers in my family go back five generations. Both my father and my grandfather were bishops in the African Methodist Episcopal (AME) church. As the pastor of an AME church in Baltimore, Maryland, I am carrying on this proud family tradition. However, this was not always so.

God was blessing me long before I realized it. I never grew up in want or deprived of any necessity. There was always food on the table, good clothes to wear, good shoes for our feet, and a solid roof over our heads. There was much prayer and Bible reading at home, and my parents modeled godly living. Even though I was raised in the church and was a "p. k." (preacher's kid), that did not stop me from wandering far afield from my roots as I grew older.

After high school, I had the opportunity to attend Yale University. By the time I entered college, I was what many would call a "party animal." Consumption of beverage alcohol consumed much of my time and attention. Although it's not something I'm proud of, I was quite a drinker then, and occasionally went on binges.

My "Bethel" came early one morning in my bed in my dormitory room at Yale, when after a drinking binge, I woke up covered in my own vomit. As I lay shaking with fear at the awareness of how easily I could have choked to death or drowned right there in my bed, God spoke to me. It wasn't an audible voice, but He definitely got my attention. "Frank, it's time to stop playing with your calling. You did not get here because you had 1600 on your SAT. You didn't get here because you got all A's in high school. You got here because I opened this door for you. And look how you waste the great privilege I gave you. Why do you keep on despising your gift and denying your call? Frank, when are you going to stop running?" He had me. I had run as far as I could run. That morning was the beginning of the turnaround in my life. God has been gracious to me beyond measure.

***

Jacob had to go to Bethel because he had to be in the right position to hear God's voice. We are the same way. There is a place for every believer where we hear God's voice. It's not necessarily a physical place, but a state of mind, an attitude, a sensitivity of spirit. We have to get into the right spiritual and mental position in order to hear God. He may have to take us to the end of our rope before we start listening, but He'll do whatever is necessary to get our attention.

Everybody has a Bethel, that place where God speaks to us clearly, where we hear His voice, and where He plants His vision in our hearts. As we enter into a new millennium, we need to look at ourselves, measure ourselves, and return to God. Our house needs to be restored, and it will happen when we go to Bethel. What happened to Jacob can happen to us. When we go to Bethel, we may walk away with a limp, but we will walk away in victory. We will never again be the same. *Everybody has a Bethel.*

Endnotes

1. Augustine, *Augustine: Confessions*; ed. and tr. Albert C. Outler, 1955, public domain. Book 8, Chapter XII, Sections 29-30. 11/9/99 <http://ccel.org/a/augustine/confessions/confessions-bod.html>

2. Martin Luther, *Luther's Tower Experience: Martin Luther Discovers the True Meaning of Righteousness*; from the preface to the Complete Edition of Luther's Latin Works, tr. Andrew Thornton, © 1983, Saint Anselm Abbey. 11/9/99 <http://www.iclnet.org/pub/resources/text/wittenberg/luther/tower.txt>

3. Al Rogers, "Amazing Grace: The Story of John Newton"; reprinted from "Away Here in Texas," July-August 1996 issue.

11/8/99 <http://members.tripod.com/~cockatoo/amazing_grace.html>

4. John Wesley, *The Journal of John Wesley*, entry for Tuesday, January 24, 1738. 11/8/99 <http://www.ccel.org/w/wesley/journal/journal.htm>

5. John Wesley, *The Journal of John Wesley*, entry for Wednesday, May 24, 1738.

6. Will Gravely, "You Must Not Kneel Here," *Christian History*, Carol Stream, IL: Christianity Today, Inc., Issue 62, vol. XVIII, no. 2, p. 34.

CHAPTER FIVE

It's Time to Clean House

Are you one of the millions of Americans who observe the annual ritual known as "spring-cleaning"? It's good periodically to busy ourselves getting rid of the dirt and dust, the grit and grime, the mold and mildew that have accumulated over the months. Isn't it amazing, too, how much "junk" we collect in the course of a year? That's why so many of us also observe that other springtime tradition known as a "yard sale." There's something mentally refreshing about clearing away the clutter and the cobwebs, not only from our homes but from our hearts as well.

Sometimes we need to carry out "spring-cleaning" in our Christian lives and in our churches. We get out of God's order when we allow a lot of religious "junk" to accumulate in our lives; we build up spiritual and moral baggage that weigh us down, slow our steps, and tire us out. Restoring the house of God means unloading the junk and getting rid of the baggage that the "spirit of religion" has hung on our shoulders—traditions, attitudes, and practices that have no business in our lives as Christians. This is what the writer of the Book of Hebrews means when he says:

> *Therefore we also, since we are surrounded by so great a cloud of witnesses, let us lay aside every weight, and the sin which so*

easily ensnares us, and let us run with endurance the race that is set before us, looking unto Jesus, the author and finisher of our faith, who for the joy that was set before Him endured the cross, despising the shame, and has sat down at the right hand of the throne of God (Hebrews 12:1-2).

During His public ministry, Jesus continually ran afoul of the religious leaders of the day because He tried to "clean house" spiritually. All four Gospels record how Jesus went into the temple courts, overturned the tables of the moneychangers, and drove out the animals, exclaiming, "It is written, 'My house shall be called a house of prayer,' but you have made it a 'den of thieves' " (Mt. 21:13), and "Take these things away! Do not make My Father's house a house of merchandise!" (Jn. 2:16) In His teaching, Jesus sought to strip away the cobwebs of religious tradition and ritual in order to bring back to light the true spirit, purpose, and meaning of the Law of God. We see this, for example, in the Sermon on the Mount when Jesus repeatedly used the formula, "You have heard that it was said...but *I* say to you..." (see Mt. 5:21-48).

When our spiritual house is out of order, foggy thinking takes over. We become confused, lazy, and careless, and before we know it, attitudes, behavior, and habits creep in that are contrary to God's will and way. Sometimes we "camp" where we are instead of moving out all the way to where God wants us to be. This is what happened to Jacob and his family. One day when God called Jacob to return to Bethel, Jacob found it necessary to "clean house" first.

Baggage From the Past

After Jacob reconciled with Esau, he and his family settled near the city of Shechem, which was in the land of Canaan but some miles north of Beersheba, his boyhood home. There they dwelled for perhaps as long as ten years. Chapter 34 of Genesis relates a sad and sorry tale that occurred during this time. Jacob's daughter Dinah was raped by Shechem, the son of Hamor, who was the ruler of the city of Shechem. The sexual passion of the young man Shechem was motivated by love, however, for he cared deeply for Dinah and wanted to marry her.

Shechem and Hamor came to Jacob with a proposal of marriage. Jacob's sons, however, were very angry over what had happened to Dinah, and used deceit (like father, like sons?) and treachery to exact revenge for the violation of their sister. They refused to agree to the marriage unless all the males in the city were circumcised. Circumcision was the specific sign of the covenant between God and the descendants of Abraham. So, Jacob's sons tried to cover their treachery with a pious, religious veneer. They sought to justify their actions by cloaking them in the guise of spirituality.

The young man Shechem readily agreed to be circumcised and the men of the city went along, seeing the potential material benefits of intermarriage with such a powerful and prosperous family as Jacob's. Three days after the circumcision, while the men were still sore from the procedure, Simeon and Levi, two of Dinah's full brothers, entered Shechem, killed all the males, and "rescued" Dinah. The rest of Jacob's sons plundered the city and enslaved the women and children. When Jacob rebuked Simeon and Levi for making him "obnoxious" to the other inhabitants of the region and for endangering the family's security, his sons simply replied, "Should he treat our sister like a harlot?" (see Genesis 34:30-31)

Why didn't Jacob rebuke his sons' treacherous and murderous actions themselves, instead of simply their negative consequences? Did he have no spiritual influence in their lives? Clearly something was wrong in the family. Jacob's spiritual house was out of order. Although Jacob worshiped and served God alone, this was apparently not the case with everyone in his household. His sons certainly had a lot to learn about the nature of God, and most of the servants in the house were probably pagans. At any rate, a lot of spiritual baggage had accumulated during the years near Shechem; the "cobwebs" were everywhere. It was time to "clean house."

Remembering Our Purpose

Then God said to Jacob, "Arise, go up to Bethel and dwell there; and make an altar there to God, who appeared to you when you fled from the face of Esau your brother" (Genesis 35:1).

Jacob endured many problems and hardships between the time of his first visit to Bethel and his return 30 years later. Under the care and providence of God, those problems and difficulties served to shape Jacob's character and lead him into maturity as the man he was destined to be in the Lord. Jacob would never have become the man God could use without the testing and proving fires of adversity.

This brings up an important truth about problems. Like it or not, problems are an inescapable part of life. They can either make us or break us; they can either shape us or shatter us. As the children of God, we are people of destiny. God created us for a purpose. We are not accidents or afterthoughts. He has a great destiny in store for us. "For I know the thoughts that I think toward you, says the Lord, thoughts of peace and not of evil, to give you a future and a hope" (Jer. 29:11). The problems that come into our lives are part of the process we must go through to realize our destiny. It is not an issue of whether or not we will have problems, but whether or not we will allow our problems to distract us from God's destiny for us. God allows problems to come into our lives in order to move us toward His purpose.

The house of God is where the children of God gather on a regular basis to remember that they are people of destiny and that God's purpose is greater than any problem they may face. One sign that we are out of order as a church is when we begin to focus on our problems instead of on the One who is greater than those problems. We lose sight of the presence, power, and purpose of God in our midst and feel defeated by the magnitude of our difficulties. On the other hand, we show spiritual maturity when we understand that even our problems and our pain have a purpose in God's design. When we look at them through His eyes we can understand what the apostle Paul meant when he said "in everything give thanks;

for this is the will of God in Christ Jesus for you" (1 Th. 5:18). This doesn't mean necessarily that we thank God for the *problem*. For example, if we had cancer, we probably wouldn't thank God *for* the disease. We *could*, however, thank God *in* the cancer because we know that through that experience He will teach us something that will make us stronger and better. When we are in order, even our problems become opportunities to give glory to God.

As Jacob learned to trust and follow the Lord, his problems and challenges served to make him strong. Then, when the time was right, God appeared to Jacob again and reminded Jacob of his purpose: "Arise, go up to Bethel and dwell there; and make an altar there to God." Remembering his purpose helped Jacob put his problems in perspective. Then he could understand that his problems were insignificant compared to the purpose and promises of God for his life. This was David's attitude when he said, "Weeping may endure for a night, but joy comes in the morning" (Ps. 30:5b). It is a matter of perspective.

The same is true with us. When God sets to work to restore our house, He will remind us of our purpose, and that reminder will put our problems into the proper perspective. God's purpose for Jacob was that he "make an altar." Likewise, God's purpose for us is that we be builders: building up one another in Christ, building a strong spiritual house, building a godly culture, and taking in people who have been torn down by the world and building them up in the Lord.

Cleaning Our House

And Jacob said to his household and to all who were with him, "Put away the foreign gods that are among you, purify your-selves, and change your garments. Then let us arise and go up to Bethel; and I will make an altar there to God, who answered me in the day of my distress and has been with me in the way which I have gone." So they gave Jacob all the foreign gods which were in their hands, and the earrings which were in their ears; and Jacob hid them under the terebinth tree which was by Shechem (Genesis 35:2-4).

Before Jacob and his household could make the journey to Bethel, they had to do some "spring-cleaning." There was a pile of "religious" junk to be thrown out and a lot of spiritual sin baggage to be unloaded and abandoned. They had to take time to cleanse themselves body, mind, and spirit.

First, they had to "put away the foreign gods" that were among them. God will brook no rivals. When our spiritual house is in order, we will neither have nor tolerate any substitutes for God. He alone is to be the object of our love, our praise, and our devotion. Before our house can be restored, we must "put away" anything that has a higher place in our affection and allegiance than God. He and He alone must reign in our hearts.

Next, Jacob and his company had to purify themselves and change their garments. This is more than simply bathing and putting on clean clothes. Before they could go to Bethel, they had to get rid of the dirt in their lives, both body and mind. In the spiritual sense, this refers to repentance, or a change of heart and mind. We can't return to Bethel until we turn our hearts and minds away from the things of the world and focus them on the things of God.

One of the major reasons so many churches are out of order is because so much of the spirit of the world has gotten inside that there is no room for the Spirit of God. Part of this worldly spirit is the "spirit of religion" that confuses and deceives a "dead" church into thinking it has life. Empty ritual, tradition, and legalism act as a counterfeit for the fullness of life in the Spirit. A "religious" spirit endows a church with a "form of godliness" which denies true spiritual power (see 2 Tim. 3:5).

Another worldly spirit that has brought disorder to much of the house of God today is the "spirit of division." One of satan's oldest and most successful strategies against the Church is "divide and conquer." When he sets us to quarreling and fighting among ourselves, we take our eyes off of God, then our power and effectiveness are diminished because we are not working together in the unity and harmony of the Spirit. Jesus said that a "house divided against itself will not stand" (Mt. 12:25b). Ironically, in context Jesus was talking about *satan's* kingdom in answering the charge that He was casting out demons by the power of the devil. The principle, however, is sound for the Church. Satan knows that if he can divide us, he can weaken us.

The "spirit of division" destroys a church's order because it creates multiple "visions" competing with each other to be the guiding principle for the church. If a church has more than one "vision," it is certain that *someone* is out of step with the Spirit; the whole church may be. The only valid vision for a church is the vision that Christ reveals because He is the head of the Church, and the only way we can know that vision is to come together in humility and ask Him to show us. Our responsibility is to embrace His vision and work together in His power to bring it about. If we are divided, it is because we are not submissive to the vision that God has for our house. That division opens a gate for the enemy to come in and beat up on us and tear us down.

A third worldly spirit that we need to clean out is the "spirit of negativity." Negativity will kill a church more quickly than just about anything else. "We can't start *that* ministry; we don't have the money." "We tried that once before and it didn't work. Why bother?" "We've never done it that way before." Negativity saps energy, quenches enthusiasm, and feeds discouragement. A negative spirit focuses on the "impossible" and constantly harps at us about what we *can't* do. It stops us from being all that God wants us to be. Our God is the God of infinite *possibilities*. "The things which are impossible with men are possible with God" (Lk. 18:27); "For with God nothing will be impossible" (Lk. 1:37); "I, the Lord, have spoken it, and I will do it" (Ezek. 36:36b); "I can do all things through Christ who strengthens me" (Phil. 4:13).

If we want our house to be restored, we must repent of our worldliness and clean out the "spirits of religion, division, and negativity" that are eating away at us. There is another worldly spirit, however, that is even more deadly than these three—the "spirit of prostitution."

Prostituting the Church

Before leaving for Bethel, Jacob told the members of his household to, "Put away the foreign gods that are among you" (Gen. 35:2b). Bethel was the "house of God," and it was unthinkable to Jacob to bring "foreign gods" or idols into God's house. Centuries later God Himself would codify this understanding by instructing the Israelites through Moses: "You shall have no other gods before Me. You shall not make for yourself a carved image..." (Ex. 20:3-4). Despite this injunction, the nation of Israel violated those commandments repeatedly, bringing upon themselves the severe judgment of God. Throughout the Old Testament, idolatry among the Israelites is described as "spiritual adultery"—the prostituting of God's people before pagan idols. Sometimes this idolatry involved literal sexual immorality with temple prostitutes, but the overall image speaks of spiritual unfaithfulness. The Book of Hosea refers to the nation of Israel as having "committed great harlotry by departing from the Lord" (Hos. 1:2b). The people had turned their backs on God and embraced the world.

Another reason so much of the house of God is out of order today is because so many of the people of God are "playing the harlot" with the world. Many of us are prostituting ourselves spiritually and aren't even aware of it. Prostitution can be described as going after a good feeling without responsibility. That's exactly what countless numbers of us do in church, Sunday after Sunday. We get all excited for the Lord to touch us and bless us and make us feel good, but we're not interested in living for Him during the week. We want the warmth of feeling without the warfare of faith, the pleasures of the prize without the rigors of the race. Like spiritual "junkies" we seek our weekly gospel "fix" so that we can go back and live like the world the rest of the time. We dress like the world, talk like the world, act like the world, and then wonder why we have no real power in our lives. We "kiss up" to the world and then complain because we're so miserable.

Church, it's time to wake up! We've been sleeping with prostitutes! Jesus said that no one can serve two masters. Either we serve God or we serve the world; there is no other option. No one says it any plainer than James:

> *Where do wars and fights come from among you? Do they not come from your desires for pleasure that war in your members? You lust and do not have. You murder and covet and cannot obtain. You fight and war. Yet you do not have because you do not ask. You ask and do not receive, because you ask amiss, that you may spend it on your pleasures. Adulterers and adulteresses! Do you not know that friendship with the world is enmity with God? Whoever therefore wants to be a friend of the world makes himself an enemy of God* (James 4:1-4).

If we sleep with prostitutes long enough, we will get spiritually transmitted diseases. We've got to clean house and break off our "friendship" with the world. We can't go to "Bethel" carting around a bunch of "foreign gods."

Selling Ourselves Cheaply

There's another way the Church prostitutes itself before the world. Sometimes we sell ourselves to the world too cheaply. We "go along to get along." Suppose, for example, that as a Christian minister, I am invited to pray at the dedication of a new public school, but in the interest of "political correctness" and to avoid offending anyone, officials ask me to offer a "general" prayer rather than to pray exclusively in the name of Jesus. If I "go along to get along," I am guilty of prostituting my faith because as Christians we are commanded to pray in Jesus' name. Christ is the head and Lord of the Church. He bought us and saved us with His own blood. If we do not pray in Jesus' name, we have no authority or reason for prayer.

This should not be offensive to the Jewish or Muslim communities. After all, if a rabbi or imam were asked to pray, I would not expect either of them to offer a prayer in Jesus' name; I would expect them to pray according to the dictates of their respective faiths. As Christians, we should be afforded the same freedom. Yet, time after time, we are faced with the challenge or expectation to "tone down" our message in order to "get along," to soft-pedal our convictions in order to keep from ruffling someone's feathers.

We prostitute our faith every time we fail to stand up for the things of God on our jobs or in our communities. We prostitute prayer whenever we fail to show the world that prayer is a precious and important thing to us. We have given in so many times and in so many ways that in the eyes of many unbelievers the Church has become inconsequential. They see the Church as having little relevance and even less influence in society and daily life. My brothers and sisters, we should hang our heads in shame and fall to our knees in repentance!

Much has been said in recent years about the separation of church and state. Anyone who has studied American history understands that the separation of church and state never meant that the churches did not have the right to speak prophetically in the public forum. This is where so much of the prostitution of the Church comes in—by and large the Church has ceased to speak prophetically to the nation. We want so badly to "fit in" and not turn people off that we have stopped proclaiming the counsels and judgments of God, which a lost and dying people desperately need to hear. Instead, in hopes of being "accepted," we compromise our convictions and water down our message to the point where they make no difference in anyone's lives, our own included. May God forgive us!

We need to follow the example of Jacob's household. When Jacob told them to give up their foreign gods, purify themselves, and change their garments, they obeyed. It was their obedience that made them ready to press forward to Bethel and all that God had in store for them. Their foreign gods, their earrings, and all other objects related to their pagan worship were gathered together and buried. Jacob's household made a clean break with the past; they let go of all that would hold them back. If we want to see the house of God restored, we must also make a clean break with the things of the world that have gotten a grip on our lives, and press ahead in humility and faith into the purposes of God.

Pressing On

And they journeyed, and the terror of God was upon the cities that were all around them, and they did not pursue the sons of Jacob. So Jacob came to Luz (that is, Bethel), which is in the land of Canaan, he and all the people who were with him. And he built an altar there and called the place El Bethel, because there God appeared to him when he fled from the face of his brother (Genesis 35:5-7).

As Jacob and his company traveled to Bethel, they discovered that the Lord was traveling with them and ahead of them. The "terror of God" fell upon the surrounding cities so that anyone who might have harbored thoughts of pursuing and attacking the travelers dared not do so because of the presence of the Lord protecting them. In reality, the Lord was with them all the time, but their ability to see His presence improved greatly once they got rid of the confusing and distracting baggage of their "foreign gods." They were then able to give undivided attention and devotion to the God who had led them safely so far. Not only did God go with them, He moved proactively on their behalf, protecting them by causing others to fear coming after them.

So Jacob and his group pressed ahead and came to Bethel where Jacob built an altar, renewing the vow he had made to the Lord years before and acknowledging the continuing nature of God's covenant with him. For Jacob it was a renewal of vision and purpose.

Likewise, when we "clean house" spiritually, we will be able to recognize God's presence with us in a way we couldn't before. We will realize that He was there all the time, but our vision was clouded by all the cobwebs and clutter. Once we put away our "foreign gods" and focus on the Lord with undivided hearts, we will have confidence to move forward, knowing that He not only is with us but goes before us.

Once we clean house and begin to walk once more in the purpose of God; once we identify and purify ourselves from the "spirits of religion, division, negativity, and prostitution"; once we recognize again the presence of God; we will be ready to press our way through. The presence of God does not mean that we don't have to press through to fulfill His purpose. God may have prepared the way, but Jacob and his household still had to travel to Bethel. We can't stay where we are and enter into God's purpose. We must move forward, leaving behind the regrets, mistakes, fears, and empty pursuits of the past. We must not let fear of the challenges and difficulties that lie ahead keep us from going forward. It is *as we go* that we will discover that God will fight our battles for us. When we are in God's order, God will fight our battles.

The apostle Paul had the right attitude. He knew nothing could be done about the past; the present walk and future glory in God's presence and purpose were all that mattered. That's why he wrote to the Philippians:

> *But what things were gain to me, these I have counted loss for Christ. Yet indeed I also count all things loss for the excellence of the knowledge of Christ Jesus my Lord, for whom I have suffered the loss of all things, and count them as rubbish, that I may gain Christ and be found in Him, not having my own righteousness, which is from the law, but that which is through faith in Christ, the righteousness which is from God by faith; that I may know Him and the power of His resurrection, and the fellowship of His sufferings, being conformed to His death, if, by any means, I may attain to the resurrection from the dead. Not that I have already attained, or am already perfected; but I press on, that I may lay hold of that for which Christ Jesus has also laid hold of me. Brethren, I do not count myself to have apprehended; but one thing I do, forgetting those things which are behind and reaching forward to those things which are*

ahead, I press toward the goal for the prize of the upward call of God in Christ Jesus (Philippians 3:7-14).

Paul's rallying cry could have been, "Onward and upward!" He was determined to press ahead to the "prize of the upward call of God in Christ Jesus." In order to grasp that prize, he first had to let go of the things from the past that he had once considered so important: his racial purity and pride, his thorough theological training, his religious discipline and devotion. It was not easy for a proud Pharisee to let go of such things. Paul had to learn to sacrifice his past, his pride, and his self-sufficiency on the altar of a heart humbled before God. He had to be broken, before God could make him whole.

Brokenness is an indispensable part of cleaning our spiritual house. The only kind of people God can restore and use are *broken* people—people who in humility recognize their utter dependence upon God for everything. We must be prepared for God to *break* us in order to *remake* us. Before our house can be restored, we must rebuild the altar of our heart and offer up ourselves to God as "living sacrifices." *Cleaning house means building an altar.*

CHAPTER SIX

Portable Altars

S ome years ago when I was pastoring in Los Angeles, a woman who had recently joined our church came to me and asked me to pray for her husband. I'll call him "Mike." During worship one Sunday morning about six to eight months later, I was in the middle of my sermon when Mike suddenly rushed to the altar shouting loudly and vociferously in the Spirit of God. He couldn't even wait for the invitation to be given. It was unusual to say the least. Mike gave his heart to Christ that morning, joined the church, and immediately became very active in the congregation. He was there for every Bible study, every prayer meeting—every time the doors were open.

About three months later I received a phone call from Mike. In an apologetic tone he asked me if I would go to court with him. Surprised, I asked him why.

"Pastor," he began, "I used to be one of the major drug dealers in this city and ended up getting hooked on my own product. I've been in prison three or four times, and now the judge is getting ready to send me away for about 20 years."

"Why didn't you tell me this when you first joined the church?"

"I was embarrassed. I know how many folks facing jail time join the church and tell their pastors that they have changed, but this is real in my life."

On the appointed date Mike entered the courtroom with his addiction therapist—and me. That was all; Mike had no lawyer. After first hearing from Mike's addiction therapist, the judge then said to Mike, "Your pastor can't speak to this issue. I'm tired of these jailhouse conversions and confessions. I don't want to hear from him, and I don't want to hear from you about it, either."

Mike jumped up and replied boldly, "Listen, Judge, I know you have the power to send me to prison for a long time and I respect that, but I will not let you disrespect my faith and my relationship with God. You don't have ultimate power over me anyway—God does. If you send me to prison, I will simply work to build the Church of Christ in prison. If you don't, I will be in church dedicating my life to Christ and working fully for Him and His Kingdom."

Silence fell in the courtroom. The judge's face turned red and he looked long and hard at Mike. *That's it*, I thought. *He's going to put Mike away for 20 years*. I just knew it.

Finally, the judge said, "I believe you. I'm going to send you back out on parole, but if you ever appear before me again, you *will* go to prison for 20 years."

Mike went on to coordinate and build a highly effective Christian substance abuse ministry in the city. Since then he has entered the ministry and is now the pastor of a rapidly growing church in a multicultural section of the greater Los Angeles area.

What made the difference for Mike? He had to reach bottom before he looked up. He was addicted and busted, trapped on a one-way street to self-destruction. Thoroughly broken, he turned to God and God lifted him up. When Mike received the grace and mercy of God, he built an altar in his heart and sacrificed on it everything that related to his old life. Forgetting what lay behind him, Mike pressed forward "toward the goal for the prize of the upward call of God in Christ Jesus" (Phil. 3:14). When Mike built an altar, God came and restored Mike's spiritual house. God wants to restore our house too, but He requires something of us. *Our part is to build an altar.*

Altar of the Heart

Then God said to Jacob, "Arise, go up to Bethel and dwell there; and make an altar there to God, who appeared to you when you fled from the face of Esau your brother."... So Jacob came to Luz (that is, Bethel), which is in the land of Canaan, he and all the people who were with him. And he built an altar there and called the place El Bethel, because there God appeared to him when he fled from the face of his brother (Genesis 35:1,6-7).

God told Jacob to do three things: return to Bethel, settle there, and build an altar. Bethel, the "house of God," represented the presence of God, the place of intimate fellowship. Jacob was to "dwell there." God's purpose for us also is that we "dwell" in intimate fellowship with Him. He wants us to abide in His presence always. That is the only way we can fulfill our destiny in God's will. Outside of an ongoing, abiding relationship with the Lord, we are powerless and ineffectual. This is what Jesus meant when He said, "Abide in Me, and I in you. As the branch cannot bear fruit of itself, unless it abides in the vine, neither can you, unless you abide in Me. I am the vine, you are the branches. He who abides in Me, and I in him, bears much fruit; for without Me you can do nothing" (Jn. 15:4-5). Christ wants our relationship to be as intimate with and dependent upon Him as that of a branch to the vine.

Jacob was to return to Bethel and build an altar. The altar is a place of worship, a place of sacrifice, a place where vows are made and fulfilled. If we desire intimacy with God, we need to build an altar. No one else can build it for us; we each must build our own. I'm not talking about a physical structure of stone that is limited to one spot, but a spiritual altar in our hearts that we take with us wherever we go. When we build an altar in our hearts, we can come into the presence of God not only at church but also at home; at school and at the workplace; at the grocery store and at the mall; at the gym and at the restaurant.

A spiritual altar of the heart is more than a place; it is God in us. Some folks *act* like they love God on Sunday, but you couldn't tell it by the way they act the rest of the week. Spirituality is not just a "Sunday thing," but a way of life. It is not something we can put on and take off like a jacket. When we abide in Christ, when we have built an altar in our hearts, we don't need anyone to tell us when it is time to pray or praise or worship. Every time we come into the divine presence and begin talking about the goodness and the glory of God, something happens to us on the inside. All it takes is the mention of the name of Jesus and we are ready to worship. Building an altar in our hearts means that we are ready and willing to love, worship, and serve the Lord *all* the time, every day, and in every walk and circumstance of life. Restoring our spiritual house means rebuilding the altar of our heart. That altar is first and foremost a *spiritual* place.

Life in Death

The basic function of an altar is as a place of sacrifice. Animal sacrifices were a central part of Hebrew worship practices, representing God's forgiveness of the people and His cleansing of their sins through the poured-out blood of an innocent lamb. The Jewish sacrificial system looked ahead to the time when Jesus Christ, the sinless Son of God, would be offered up on the altar of the cross as the ultimate, once-and-for-all sacrifice for sin. In the words of John the Baptist, Jesus was "the Lamb of God who takes away the sin of the world" (Jn. 1:29b). There is no forgiveness without sacrifice, no salvation without the spilling of sinless blood. Hebrews 9:22b says, "without shedding of blood there is no remission." That remission comes through the sacrificial death of Christ: "In Him we have redemption through His blood, the forgiveness of sins..." (Eph. 1:7).

An altar, then, is a place of death. Animals sacrificed as sin offerings were given over totally to God—completely consumed—on the altar. Building an altar in our heart requires our death as well—not physical death, but death to self: death to self-will, self-ambition, and self-sufficiency. There is no other way to walk with the Lord. It is only in *dying* that we can discover what it really means to *live*. This is what the apostle Paul meant when he wrote, "I have been crucified with Christ; it is no longer I who live, but Christ lives in me; and the life which I now live in the flesh I live by faith in the Son of God, who loved me and gave Himself for me" (Gal. 2:20). God is looking for people who are willing to lay down their lives on the altar of sacrifice and allow Him to live *His* life *in* and *through* them. Paul had this in mind when he wrote to the Romans, "I beseech you therefore, brethren, by the mercies of God, that you *present your bodies a living sacrifice*, holy, acceptable to God, which is your reasonable service" (Rom. 12:1, emphasis added).

When we build an altar in our hearts and lay down our lives on it, God will take us through a cleansing, consuming fire that will burn up everything that is not of Him. Everything old, corrupt, and sinful will be burned away leaving only that which is pure, holy, and righteous. "For He is like a refiner's fire and like launderers' soap. He will sit as a refiner and a purifier of silver; He will purify the sons of Levi, and purge them as gold and silver, that they may offer to the Lord an offering in righteousness" (Mal. 3:2b-3).

This is one way to look at the problems we face in life. While it is certainly true that we bring many problems upon ourselves by our own foolish choices or sinful actions, many others come our way through no fault of our own. These difficulties can either make us or break us, depending on our attitude. If we let Him, God can use our difficulties to make us strong. Simon Peter understood this when he wrote, "In this you greatly rejoice, though now for a little while, if need be, you have been grieved by various trials, that the genuineness of your faith, being much more precious than gold that perishes, though it is tested by fire, may be found to praise, honor, and glory at the revelation of Jesus Christ" (1 Pet. 1:6-7).

One of the problems in the Church today is that we want blessings without sacrifice. It doesn't work that way. There is no blessing without sacrifice. Something has to die. The reason most of us do not walk in the full blessings of God is because we are not willing to die. We lack spiritual wisdom, insight, and power because we are afraid to die. We do not live in the spiritual realm because we refuse to die to the worldly realm. All of us have things that need to die: sinful habits, worldly relationships, lustful thought patterns. These are characteristics of "the old man which grows corrupt according to the deceitful lusts" (Eph. 4:22b). We need to "be renewed in the spirit of [our] mind, and...put on the new man which was created according to God, in true righteousness and holiness" (Eph. 4:23-24). If we lay aside the old life in order to take up "the mind of Christ" (1 Cor. 2:16b), God will raise us up to new levels of blessing and glory. But we have to die first. In God's Kingdom, life is found in death. Jesus said, "If anyone desires to come after Me, let him deny himself, and take up his cross, and follow Me. For whoever desires to save his life will lose it, but whoever loses his life for My sake will find it" (Mt. 16:24b-25).

Made for Sacrifice

Much of the Church in America today is facing a male gender crisis. What I mean is that in many churches and denominations, active, committed men are getting harder and harder to find. The Church has lost its appeal for many men. One reason for this, I believe, is that so many of our churches have stopped emphasizing the sacrificial element of faith. We focus more attention on what *we* can get and on having *our* needs met than we do on what we can *give* to God and how we can *serve* others in His name. Much of modern American church life is selfish.

Men are made for sacrifice; it's in our nature. That's one reason why we go to war. With all of its blood, sacrifice, camaraderie, hardship, and heroism, war is a rite of passage for men. Whether they realize it or not, most men are looking for something to give themselves to sacrificially. Many find it through devoting long, hard hours on the job to support their families, and giving much time to community activities and service. Men who cannot find traditional outlets through work, family, community, or church often dissipate their sacrificial drive in self-destructive ways: gangs, alcohol, drugs, crime, deliberate risk-taking and "thrill-seeking." Recovering the sacrificial element of faith is a critical key to restoring the house of God as well as restoring men to the house of God.

The Church needs to find new ways to motivate men to rise to the challenge of a sacrificial life in Christ. Many men may be somewhat put off by some of the "feminine" metaphors in the Church. For example, the Church is the "bride" of Christ. Of course, this is a biblical concept that is true in the spiritual sense and needs to be taught. Such a metaphor, however, may not speak as well to men in general as it does to women. Some men may respond better to a different image, one that is more "masculine." The New Testament refers to believers as "sons of God":

But as many as received Him, to them gave He power to become the sons of God, even to them that believe on His name (John 1:12 KJV).

For as many as are led by the Spirit of God, these are sons of God (Romans 8:14).

For you are all sons of God through faith in Christ Jesus (Galatians 3:26).

Understanding that we are *sons* of God connects us to the *Son* of God who lived a life of sacrifice. That connection challenges us to live sacrificially as well, with Christ Himself as our example. When the Church once again holds up the sacrificial example of Jesus before the world, lost people will be attracted to Him. Many men will be brought or restored to the house of God. Jesus said, "And I, if I am lifted up from the earth, will draw all peoples to Myself" (Jn. 12:32).

While the call to sacrifice may have a special appeal to men, the challenge to sacrificial living is extended to all. Any person, man or woman, boy or girl, who is willing to submit himself or herself to God as a living sacrifice becomes a person God can use. Age doesn't matter. Educational level doesn't matter and neither does economic status. What matters is *willingness*. God will use people who are willing to be used and who make themselves available to Him. That's the essence of sacrificial living, being *willing* and *available*. It means learning to die to self so that Christ can rule supremely. Living sacrificially means willing *submission* to become *broken vessels* whom God has restored and fitted for His use.

Broken Vessels

The altar is a place of submission where we acknowledge the absolute sovereignty and holiness of God, and where we lay down all rights and claims to ourselves. Whatever we lay on the altar of our heart must be our very best, because only our very best is acceptable to God. In the Old Testament, animals suitable for sacrifice to God had to be without flaw or blemish. They had to be valuable to their owners. Giving that which costs us nothing is not a sacrifice. Offering to God that which we can do without is not a sacrifice. Letting go of what we can afford is not a sacrifice. What we render to God reveals how we truly feel about Him and how much value we place on our relationship with Him. Anything less than our best is an insult to God and will never lead to His blessings. The very best we have to offer God is *ourselves*, whole and complete. He expects and demands nothing less.

God commanded Abraham to take that which was most precious to him, his son Isaac, and to offer him as a sacrifice. God said to Abraham, "Give Me your very best." As Abraham submitted himself to God and raised the knife to slay his son, God stayed his hand, saying, "Do not lay your hand on the lad, or do anything to him; for now I know that you fear God, since you have not withheld your son, your only son, from Me" (Gen. 22:12). Then the Lord provided a ram to be sacrificed in Isaac's place. When Abraham submitted to the divine will, he came to know God as *Jehovah-Jireh*, "the Lord our Provider." Abraham's submission led to a greater knowledge of God, resulting in deeper intimacy with Him.

During the 30 years between his trips to Bethel, Jacob learned to submit to God's will and leadership in his life. He laid down his self-will, his ambition, and his self-sufficiency, and learned to depend on and follow God. In a very real sense, God "broke" Jacob of who he was, then reassembled the pieces, making Jacob into someone new. Jacob was a "broken vessel" who was restored and fitted for his Master's purpose. After he wrestled with God and pressed through for his blessing, Jacob even carried away with him a lifelong limp as a sign and reminder of his brokenness.

Walking with God is a glorious experience but not an easy one. If we press through as Jacob did, we will eventually receive our blessing, but we have to realize that somewhere along the way God is going to break something. Blessings don't come without brokenness. We may end up with a broken heart, a broken relationship, broken finances; but if we cling to God, He will restore us in our brokenness. God has to break us in order to bless us. Did your life fall apart just when you thought you had it all together? Perhaps God broke you to teach you to depend on a power and a wisdom greater than your own. Did your marriage fail or your best friend betray you? In that brokenness God may want you to learn to rely on Him, and not on anyone else. Did your finances collapse? Maybe God broke you to teach you that money isn't everything.

Brokenness is a necessary part of altar building. An altar is a place of worship. Only those who are humble can worship God, and brokenness fosters humility. It was King David who, in the midst of brokenness and shame over his sins of adultery with Bathsheba and the murder of her husband, Uriah, wrote, "The sacrifices of God are a broken spirit, a broken and a contrite heart; these, O God, You will not despise" (Ps. 51:17). In his brokenness, David humbled himself before God, repented, and was restored.

The People God Uses

God specializes in taking broken people, restoring them, and using them to accomplish His purposes, thereby bringing glory to His name. Mighty deeds performed through broken vessels leave no doubt in anyone's mind that God is at work. Remember Jacob, that rogue, thief, and liar whom God broke and then raised up to father a mighty nation.

Don't forget Joseph who, broken from Jacob's favorite son to a slave in Egypt and an inmate in pharaoh's prison, was lifted up by God to second in command under pharaoh to preserve his family and many others during a time of great famine. Consider Moses. Broken from a prince of Egypt to a lowly shepherd in the wilderness, Moses was the vessel through whom God delivered His chosen people from slavery and prepared them to enter the promised land. Remember Paul, whom God broke from a proud, self-righteous Pharisee to one who would testify, "For to me, to live is Christ and to die is gain" (Phil. 1:21), and whom God used to evangelize the Gentile world.

Only God could do these things. His glory shines brightest through our brokenness. Paul came to understand and appreciate this truth as he learned to live with his "thorn in the flesh" (see 2 Cor. 12:7). "Concerning this thing I pleaded with the Lord three times that it might depart from me. And He said to me, 'My grace is sufficient for you, for My strength is made perfect in weakness.' Therefore most gladly I will rather boast in my infirmities, that the power of Christ may rest upon me" (2 Cor. 12:8-9). Christ Himself had to be broken on the cross before He could be glorified through the resurrection. He had to die before we could receive life.

So who are the people God uses? He chooses the broken, the humbled, those who have reached the end of their own resources and have nowhere to turn but to Him. He chooses those who have sunk so far down that there is nowhere else to look except up. To put it another way, God chooses to use those who know that they stand in need of His restoration. Jesus said that the Kingdom of Heaven belongs to those who are the "poor in spirit" (see Mt. 5:3)—those who know that they are nothing in and of themselves and are without hope apart from God. In Jesus' parable of the Pharisee and the publican praying in the temple (see Lk. 18:10-14), it was not the proud Pharisee who went home right with God, but the broken publican who humbly begged for mercy. Jesus concluded that story by stating a Kingdom principle that is completely at odds with the philosophy of the world: "For everyone who exalts himself will be humbled, and he who humbles himself will be exalted" (Lk. 18:14b).

If God has broken you in some area of your life, it is because he wants to rebuild you into a vessel fit for Himself and use you for His glory. When God breaks us, we need to take that brokenness and lay it on the altar of our hearts for Him to do with as He pleases. After all, a sacrifice has no voice in how it is used. God is looking for broken people who want to be restored. If the house of God is to be restored to divine order, power, and influence, it will be through broken people who lay down at the altar their pride, their self-sufficiency, their selfish ambition, their greed, their lust—all the useless "baggage" of the world—and who offer themselves up to God as "living sacrifices" to His glory. These are the people God chooses. These are the people God uses.

Strong at the Broken Places

A broken bone that has healed is strongest at the place where the break occurred. The same is true in the spiritual realm. When we come in our brokenness to the altar and lay ourselves down in humbleness before the Lord, we will rise up and go our way stronger than when we arrived.

When I was growing up, I served as an altar boy in the church my father pastored. St. James AME Church in St. Louis, Missouri had a divided chancel. On one side was the pulpit for the preacher; on the other, a smaller lectern where announcements were given, Scripture was read, and other parts of the worship service were performed. At the front of the chancel the altar was separated from the rest of the sanctuary by a low railing with a gate at the center. One of the jobs as an altar boy was to hold the gate open for people who came forward during the invitation to pray at the altar.

My father was a strong believer in altar prayer. He extended the opportunity at every service. As an altar boy, I could hardly wait until it was my turn to hold the gate. Time after time I watched people come to the altar in tears and pray on their knees with their shoulders heaving from their sobs. Others came with their bodies and faces weighed down with great burdens. The longer I watched, the more I noticed that people who came to the altar burdened and weeping walked away a little straighter, a little taller, and a little stronger. Tear-streaked faces were then calm and at peace. I remember once asking my father, "Daddy, what happens at the altar?" I will never forget his answer. "At the altar broken people are put back together. At the altar weak people are made strong." That was why every Sunday during the altar call we sang,

> Come, ye disconsolate, where'er ye languish,
> Come to the mercy seat, fervently kneel;
> Here bring your wounded hearts, here tell your anguish:
> Earth has no sorrow that heav'n cannot heal.

Becoming a Sacrifice

Have you built an altar to God in your heart? Have you laid on it before Him your house, your relationships, your church, and your family? True spiritual strength and power are found in sacrificial living, not in religious entertainment. At one time I was a great religious "entertainer"; I knew how to make folks feel good on Sundays. After about ten years of it, however, I finally realized that the same folks who were jumping, shouting, and praising God on Sunday were depressed, unhappy, and getting beaten up by their problems on Monday. I went to God and said, "Lord, what's going on? We sing, we shout, we praise, we feel good, yet nothing seems to last. Our marriages are breaking up. Our kids are rebelling, drinking, doing drugs. A lot of folks, even some of those I baptized, are acting like they have lost their minds. Why?" His answer changed the focus of my ministry. He said, "My people don't need entertainment; they need to learn how to build altars in their lives."

The call of Christ is a call to sacrificial living. It is a call to a life of submission to the Word and the will of God. It is a call to a truly spiritual life of genuine holiness and righteousness in the power of the Spirit. As we respond to Christ's call and begin to live a truly spiritual lifestyle of sacrifice and submission, we will find ourselves strengthened in the Lord day by day and moment by moment. The result will be an undeniably powerful and influential witness in our material culture.

We live in a society that no longer believes in or values personal sacrifice or submission. Both are unwelcome concepts in a culture characterized by selfish ambition and the headlong pursuit of wealth and pleasure. So much of modern life is superficial and shallow because so few people are willing to stand up and be counted for the things that really matter. Our nation and our world desperately need to see the witness of the people of God standing firm, even giving their lives (figuratively or literally) in the name of Christ.

Sacrificial living restores intimacy with God. Without sacrifice, without submission, without a God-focused spirituality, there is no intimacy. So how do we build an altar in our hearts? We build an altar by giving ourselves to *become* that altar. A physical altar is a place given over exclusively to the worship and service of God. We are spiritual altars given over for the same purpose. Unlike a physical altar, however, we are not confined to a single spot. Instead, we are walking, talking, witnessing, working, moving, *portable altars*. We build an altar by building a *life* submitted to God. One by one, as we yield to the Lord, out of our godly lives grow godly families, and out of godly families grow godly churches. Godly churches influence the growth of godly communities out of which grows a godly nation. A godly nation can help build a godly world.

This is the destiny the Lord has for us, His people. We will not realize that destiny as long as we continue to think of ourselves as spiritual paupers. Vision of our heritage and purpose in Christ is one of the things the enemy has stolen from us. That loss of vision is one of the reasons our house is out of order and needs to be restored. When we rebuild the altars of our hearts and renew our intimacy with the Lord, He will lead us from the poverty of our own weakness and limited vision to the prosperity of His power and purpose.

CHAPTER SEVEN

From Poverty to Purpose

In *The Last Battle*, the seventh and final volume in his classic fantasy series *The Chronicles of Narnia*, C.S. Lewis depicts a powerful and original concept of Heaven. One scene is a telling commentary on the attitudes of many Christians today. Lewis's characters have just crossed over from the physical world of earth to the spiritual world of Heaven where they are encouraged to go "further up and further in" to experience paradise to its fullest extent. Just inside the boundary of Heaven they encounter a circle of dwarves seated on the ground facing each other. Totally wrapped up in themselves and their own little world, the dwarves are unaware of and unconcerned with the greater realm around them. From their point of view they are in a drab, dingy stable, and they refuse to believe that there is anything more. Nothing can induce them to go any farther or to take any interest whatsoever in what lies beyond the boundary. Content to stay where they are, they are completely blind to the greater life and fuller joy that lie "further up and further in."

Lewis's picture here is of people who are in the Kingdom of Heaven but who, due to their limited vision, fail to experience and enjoy the fullness of Kingdom life. Tradition, inadequate grounding in foundational truths, unbelief, and the wiles of satan all play a part in blinding believers to the full awareness of who they are in Christ and what they have inherited in Him. Unable to see beyond their own immediate circumstances, these believers become, in effect, "paupers in the palace."

In practical terms, this describes the daily reality of more believers than we would care to admit. Our churches are filled with people who have a very limited understanding and even less experience of the fullness of life in Christ. For many of us, the abundant life in the Spirit depicted in the New Testament is a far cry from our usual daily reality. We have lost any real sense of the presence of God, rarely experience the power of God, and consequently do not walk in the purposes of God. In short, we have lost our vision.

Whenever a church or individual believer loses intimacy with God, one consequence is the loss of vision concerning God's purpose. A house out of order is a house without vision. Proverbs 29:18 (KJV) says, "Where there is no vision, the people perish: but he that keepeth the law, happy is he." A more contemporary version of the verse reads, "Where there is no revelation, the people cast off restraint; but happy is he who keeps the law." The Hebrew verb *para* ("perish," "cast off restraint") has three basic meanings: to "let loose" in the sense of cutting or unbraiding the hair, to "let loose" in the sense of letting run wild, and to "let loose" in the sense of letting something slip through one's fingers. In this sense it also means to "ignore" or "reject." With these meanings in mind, the first part of Proverbs 29:18 could be stated this way: "Where there is no vision, the people are undisciplined/get out of hand."[1] That's a pretty accurate description of a church that is out of order!

We "get out of hand" when we go our own way and do our own thing without looking to God for His direction. When the house is restored, intimacy with God will be restored. When intimacy is restored, vision of God's purpose will be restored. If we want to see our house restored, we need to "catch the vision."

Broadening Our View

Most people, whether inside or outside the church, have the wrong concept of God. The late comic Flip Wilson used to portray a preacher's wife who frequently declared, "God's gonna get you for that!" His humorous characterization nonetheless expressed the way many people view God—as a harsh and vindictive judge just waiting to pounce on us and "zap" us for the least infraction. This idea stems largely from the tradition of "hellfire and brimstone" preachers and from Christian sects and denominations that focus on the legalistic and judgmental aspects of faith.

At the opposite extreme are the people who are in the "God is love" camp, who view God as a jovial, jolly "Santa Claus" type, a doting grandfatherly deity who winks at the childish mischief and escapades of His children and overlooks their weaknesses and mistakes. Those who see God this way cannot conceive how a "loving" God could possibly bring judgment or other "cruel" things against people.

While there are elements of truth in both views, neither one gives a complete picture. Certainly, God does execute judgment against sin. After all, He is holy, righteous, and just, and cannot abide the presence of evil and corruption. However, He is also a God of grace, love, mercy, and compassion. The same God who declares that "the soul who sins shall die" (Ezek. 18:20a) also says, "I have loved you with an everlasting love" (Jer. 31:3b). The same Bible that states, "Behold, the day of the Lord comes, cruel, with both wrath and fierce anger, to lay the land desolate; and He will destroy its sinners from it" (Is. 13:9) also says, "The Lord is gracious and full of compassion, slow to anger and great in mercy. The Lord is good to all, and His tender mercies are over all His works" (Ps. 145:8-9).

We need to change and broaden our view of God. He takes no delight in judgment; He would much rather bless. "Say to them: 'As I live,' says the Lord God, 'I have no pleasure in the death of the wicked, but that the wicked turn from his way and live. Turn,

turn from your evil ways! For why should you die, O house of Israel?' " (Ezek. 33:11) God wants to bless, not curse. Whichever one we receive from God's hand depends on the choices *we* make.

When the nation of Israel was poised to enter the promised land, Moses warned them of the critical choice that lay before them. "Behold, I set before you today a blessing and a curse: the blessing, if you obey the commandments of the Lord your God which I command you today; and the curse, if you do not obey the commandments of the Lord your God, but turn aside from the way which I command you today, to go after other gods which you have not known" (Deut. 11:26-28). The subsequent history of Israel reveals that more often than not they made choices that brought God's curse upon them.

God wants to bless us, but too often we bring judgment or negative consequences upon ourselves by the choices we make. For example, God has given us standards for proper sexual behavior both as a protection for us and to ensure that we can fully enjoy that gift within proper boundaries. If we play fast and loose with our sexual morality, however, we then have no right to blame God when we come down with syphilis or AIDS or some other sexually transmitted disease. We are simply reaping what we have sown. If our finances are messed up because we spend more money than we make or blow a lot of it buying lottery tickets, we have no right to blame God for our money problems. *We* made the choices that put us in that position. Yet so often we sit and complain about our plight and wonder why God doesn't bless us, when all along it is *our choices* that prevent Him from blessing us the way He really wants to! We need to learn how to break the yokes in our lives and walk in the joy, the power, and the peace of the Lord.

When God Shows Up

Then God appeared to Jacob again, when he came from Padan Aram, and blessed him. And God said to him, "Your name is Jacob; your name shall not be called Jacob anymore, but Israel shall be your name." So He called his name Israel (Genesis 35:9-10).

These verses reveal something of the vision of God's blessing that He wants all of us to catch. There is a direct link between God's presence and God's "presents" (blessings). "Then God appeared to Jacob again...and blessed him." Before we can be blessed, God has to show up. When God shows up to people who are trying to walk in faithful obedience to Him, blessings always follow. God's desire is to bless us "exceedingly abundantly above all that we ask or think" (Eph. 3:20). What this means is that we cannot even envision the extent or height of the blessings that God wants to pour out on us! That's how much He loves us!

So often we miss out or cut ourselves off from the blessings God wants to give us. Perhaps it is because we're grasping the things of the world and cannot hold the things of God. It may be because we're seeking God's blessings on *our* terms instead of His. We keep telling God what we want Him to do and never bother to try to find out what He wants to do. It may be because we are content to be where we are, safe in our comfort zone, asking less of God than He wants to give us. In that case, He usually gives us only as much as we ask for. He will not push us beyond where we are willing to go. Once again, *our* choices often determine the extent of the blessings we receive.

When God showed up at Bethel, He changed Jacob's life forever. "Jacob" became "Israel." There is much more involved here than a simple name change. Jacob's experience reveals two fundamental blessings that God wants all of us to have. The first of these is the blessing of *transformation.*

Fit for a King

Medieval scientists frequently devoted much of their time to alchemy, the attempt to transform base metals such as lead or iron into gold. Such efforts were doomed to failure because success would have involved altering the very nature of the metal, something even twentieth century science cannot do. Only God is capable of such a radical transformation.

No transformation is more radical than that of a sinner to a saint, yet that is precisely the business that God is about. He took Jacob the deceiver and made of him the father of a great nation. He transformed a rogue into one who would "rule as God." For Jacob the change was neither quick nor easy, but the long-term gain was worth the short-term pain. Through the fires of trial and adversity, God purged from Jacob all the "impurities" of character that kept him from becoming the man God wanted him to be.

In the same way, God wants to transform us into royal children fit to rule in His Kingdom. Like Jacob, we all have impurities that need to be removed. This does not always mean cleaning out only the sin and the worldliness in our lives. Sometimes God will purge "good" things that nevertheless stand in the way of His *best* for us. When gold is refined, impurities are burned away in accordance with the degree of purity desired in the final product. *Pure* gold, the highest and most valuable form, has every possible impurity removed. In the process of refining pure gold, the last "impurity" to be removed is *silver*. A precious metal in its own right, silver is good but gold is better. If your goal is pure gold, silver is an impurity.

God is determined to purge from our lives everything that keeps us from being pure and holy vessels for Him. He will finish what He started. As Paul assured the Philippians, "He who has begun a good work in you will complete it until the day of Jesus Christ" (Phil. 1:6b). As with Jacob, God's purging process in our lives will be neither quick nor always easy. Sometimes it will be painful. Nevertheless it is absolutely critical if we are to be restored and enter into God's holy purpose. The aim of the cleansing fire is not to break us, but to burn up everything in our lives that is worthless so that when we come out, we can testify along with Job that, "When He has tested me, I shall come forth as gold" (Job 23:10b). Just as He transformed Jacob into Israel, the one who would "rule as God," changing Jacob's character in the process, so God is transforming us from sinners into His royal children fit to rule with Him, changing our character along the way.

Victory Assured

The second fundamental blessing illustrated in Jacob's name change that God wants for us is the blessing of *triumph*. When God shows up among His faithful, obedient people, He brings victory. God doesn't make losers; He restores losers and turns them into winners. While he was still a deceiver and trickster and on the run, Jacob didn't seem to have much going for him. Then God showed up, changed Jacob's name to Israel, changed his character and his destiny, and made him a winner.

Every one of us who is a believer is a winner no matter who we were before or where we came from. God has made us champions through Jesus Christ. If we are following the Lord, not even the strongest attacks from the world can defeat us. They may knock us down, shake us up, give us a few bruises, even inflict some painful wounds, but they will never defeat us. "You are of God, little children, and have overcome them [the false spirits of the world], because He who is in you is greater than he who is in the world" (1 Jn. 4:4). Jesus said, "These things I have spoken to you, that in Me you may have peace. In the world you will have tribulation; but be of good cheer, I have overcome the world" (Jn. 16:33).

One of the consequences of getting our house out of order and losing our intimacy with God is that we run the risk of forgetting that we are champions. When that happens, we begin to concentrate on our problems and difficulties, our pains and our setbacks, and a sense of defeat sets in. Any coach worth his salt will tell you that when a team begins to feel like a loser, it quickly becomes a loser. Defeat is never far behind. Victory begins as an attitude long before it becomes a reality on the playing field. Successful coaches know that their teams must learn to think and act like champions before they will ever perform like champions.

Many of us who have lost the joy and confidence in our Christian lives have forgotten where the Lord has brought us from and where He is taking us. We need to remember those times when we felt defeated and the Lord stopped and said, "You are My child and I love you. Don't let the world tell you you're nothing or that you can't do this or can't do that. I will lift you up." Can you remember the time when you were a loser but Jesus came into your life and made you a winner? Now you can smile when you feel like frowning. You can go on when you feel like giving up because God showed up and made you triumphant.

We need to recapture that vision of triumph, because when we catch that vision, we will walk differently and talk differently. True winners *act* like winners even when the odds are against them. Champions never give up. Our character and self-image—who we are and how we see ourselves—will determine how we behave when the "crunch times" come. If we are focused on our problems and all the reasons why we *can't* succeed, the inevitable crunch times of life may break us. On the other hand, if we have the vision of God's promised victory in our spirits, when the crunch times come, we can act like champions instead of like chumps. Folks may ask us how we can be so confident in the crunch. That's when we can say with the psalmist, "Weeping may endure for a night, but joy comes in the morning" (Ps. 30:5b). When they ask us how we can remain strong amidst the pressures of life, that's when we can say with Isaiah, "But those who wait on the Lord shall renew their strength; they shall mount up with wings like eagles, they shall run and not be weary, they shall walk and not faint" (Is. 40:31).

We can be cool, calm, and confident no matter what life throws at us and no matter how much the pressure builds because in Christ we can see the *end* of the story. God has given us the vision, the promise, the blessing of *victory*!

Knowing God

Also God said to him: "I am God Almighty. Be fruitful and multiply; a nation and a company of nations shall proceed from you, and kings shall come from your body. The land which I gave Abraham and Isaac I give to you; and to your descendants after you I give this land." Then God went up from him in the place where He talked with him. So Jacob set up a pillar in the place where He talked with him, a pillar of stone; and he poured a drink offering on it, and he poured oil on it. And Jacob called the name of the place where God spoke with him, Bethel (Genesis 35:11-15).

One of the tragedies of modern church life is that while many people in our churches may know a lot *about* God, very few really *know* God in any intimate way. This explains why so many find the Bible hard to understand and why it seems so irrelevant to their situation. They may read it, but they don't know the God who wrote it. This also explains why so many Christians get torn up and beaten down by life and why the Church as a whole makes little impact on our contemporary culture.

Jacob did not just know *about* God; he *knew God* because God came and *spoke* to him. Look at the references to God speaking in the verses above: "God said to him"; "He talked with him" (twice); "God spoke with him." These words describe an intimate relationship between God and Jacob.

The reason so many of us live mediocre, plain, dull, struggling lives is because we talk about God but do not really know Him intimately. Knowing someone intimately means knowing his weaknesses as well as his strengths, his private self as well as his public self. The more we get to know God, the more we realize that He has no weaknesses; we can trust Him with complete confidence. This builds our faith. The more we get to know ourselves, the more we realize how few strengths we really have and how dependent we really are on God, who knows us better than we know ourselves. This encourages us to cast all our cares upon Him because He cares for us. The result of this interaction is a growth in intimacy. We move beyond mere *religion* into *relationship*.

Today we need to catch and realize the vision of intimacy with God if we want Him to lift us to the next level of greatness and growth in our lives and in our relationship with Him. We need to *know* God. Who *is* God? He said to Jacob, "I am God Almighty" (Hebrew: *El-Shaddai*). He is the omnipotent One, all-powerful in both Heaven and earth. He is the omniscient One, all-knowing; nothing is hidden from Him. He is the omnipresent One; there is nowhere we can go that is out of His presence and care (or judgment, as the case may be).

When we know God Almighty, we can proceed with confidence wherever He leads us. "If God is for us, who can be against us?" (Rom. 8:31b) When we know God Almighty we can accomplish whatever we put our hands to under His guidance. "I can do all things through Christ who strengthens me" (Phil. 4:13). When we know God Almighty, He will fight our battles for us. "Plead my cause, O Lord, with those who strive with me; fight against those who fight against me" (Ps. 35:1). When we know God Almighty, He will open doors for us. "I know your works. See, I have set before you an open door, and no one can shut it; for you have a little strength, have kept My word, and have not denied My name" (Rev. 3:8). When we know God Almighty, He will be our bridge over troubled water. "God is our refuge and strength, a very present help in trouble" (Ps. 46:1). When we know God Almighty, He will always be with us. "For He Himself has said, 'I will never leave you nor forsake you' " (Heb. 13:5b).

God's heart is toward the restoration of His people. He *wants* us to know Him and love Him. "Then I will give them a heart to know Me, that I am the Lord; and they shall be My people, and I will be their God, for they shall return to Me with their whole heart" (Jer. 24:7). Not only does God want us to know Him personally, He wants us to know Him with regard to His *purpose*, with regard to His *promises*, and with regard to His *presence*.

Created for a Purpose

God created each of us for a purpose. He has saved and called us deliberately. We are neither accidents nor afterthoughts in God's mind. He wants us to know our purpose and the plans He has for us. God spoke plainly regarding His purpose for Jacob: "I am God Almighty. Be fruitful and multiply; a nation and a company of nations shall proceed from you, and kings shall come from your body. The land which I gave Abraham and Isaac I give to you; and to your descendants after you I give this land" (Gen. 35:11b-12).

First of all, God told Jacob to "be fruitful and multiply." This is a direct echo of the command God originally gave to Adam and Eve. Fruitfulness in abundance is a distinguishing characteristic of the Kingdom of God because God Himself is fruitful. Just look at the splendor, beauty, glory, and limitless diversity of the created order! Fruitfulness is the natural result of life in the Spirit of God. This command was fulfilled in Jacob's life as he fathered 12 sons and at least one daughter. These children grew to have families of their own. Many generations passed until at last a great host of people—an entire nation descended from one ex-con man—stood ready to be delivered from bondage in Egypt and ushered into the "promised land" of blessing and purpose.

There is more to this command, however, than simple physical procreation. From the beginning, God has had a spiritual purpose in mind. Everything He does is redemptive in nature. God's ultimate purpose for Jacob's fruitfulness was to produce a nation of godly people through whom a Savior would come—the King of kings—who would turn the hearts of the whole world to His grace, mercy, love and forgiveness. This would fulfill God's promise to Abraham when He said, "And in you all the families of the earth shall be blessed" (Gen. 12:3b).

Just as with Jacob, God wants us to be fruitful and multiply, not just physically or materially, but spiritually. He wants us to stop thinking like paupers and settling for second best. After all, we're "King's kids." Even if you live in a ghetto or drive an old car that's about to fall apart, even if you struggle just to live from one paycheck to the next, if you've given your heart and life to Christ, then you are a child of the King. God wants all of His children to prosper. If we follow Him and obey Him, He will bless us and lead us through the tough times into the greater joy of His purpose.

God still desires for all nations to know Him. He still wants to raise up from us "nations" and "kings" for that purpose. Do you want to know what God's purpose is for you, and for all of us who are believers? Consider the words of the apostle Peter. "But you are a chosen generation, a royal priesthood, a holy nation, His own special people, that you may proclaim the praises of Him who called you out of darkness into His marvelous light; who once were not a people but are now the people of God, who had not obtained mercy but now have obtained mercy" (1 Pet. 2:9-10).

Please Pass the Promises

The promise that God gave to Jacob in Genesis 35:12 was multigenerational in scope. "The land which I gave Abraham and Isaac I give to you; and to your descendants after you I give this land." Once we catch the vision of God's purpose, we understand that His wonderful promises are not for us alone, but for our children and our children's children. God wants to bless not only us, but also the next generation, and the next, and the next, and the next....

Our responsibility is great. Not only must we learn to live and walk in God's promises for us, but we must also be careful to teach these things to the next generation so that they too can know the promises of God and walk in intimate fellowship with Him. They in turn must teach the next generation, and so pass down the generational blessing.

One reason so many of our houses and lives are out of order is because we have forgotten the promises of God and therefore failed to pass them on to our children. It seems as though in our society each generation tends to be more individualistic and selfish than the preceding one. So many people today are focused on "me," getting "my" share, striving to get more and more things that they can consume on their own selfish desires. In many quarters there is little thought for tomorrow; the focus is on the "now" of "eat, drink, and be merry, for tomorrow we die." When this attitude takes root in the Church, the results can be disastrous. Instead of blessings, we pass on curses and raise up a generation of people who do not know God.

Generational blessings are not about what we spend on our own lusts and desires, but what we invest for the generations coming after us so that they can know God, love God, and serve God, and experience even greater blessings than we do. It is so easy to pass on a curse rather than a blessing. All we have to do is keep reinforcing negative choices or circumstances. "You're just like your no-good daddy. He never amounted to anything, and neither will you." When we pound negativity on our children, we set them up to fail. We destroy their self-esteem and our negative words become self-fulfilling prophecies.

We have a God-given responsibility to teach our children that God loves them and to help them learn how to love Him in return and give their lives to Him. God has charged us to pass on to them the legacy of who they are in Him and an awareness of all the vast riches of glory that are theirs as children of God. The Bible is filled with precious promises for God's people. Imagine what could happen in our lives and those of our children if we would simply feed regularly on morsels such as these:

> *For I know the thoughts that I think toward you, says the Lord, thoughts of peace and not of evil, to give you a future and a hope. Then you will call upon Me and go and pray to Me, and I will listen to you. And you will seek Me and find Me, when you search for Me with all your heart* (Jeremiah 29:11-13).

> *And my God shall supply all your need according to His riches in glory by Christ Jesus* (Philippians 4:19).

> *But as it is written: "Eye has not seen, nor ear heard, nor have entered into the heart of man the things which God has prepared for those who love Him"* (1 Coronthians 2:9).

> *Trust in the Lord, and do good; dwell in the land, and feed on His faithfulness. Delight yourself also in the Lord, and He shall give you the desires of your heart. Commit your way to the Lord, trust also in Him, and He shall bring it to pass. He shall bring forth your righteousness as the light, and your justice as the noonday* (Psalm 37:3-6).

> *For you shall go out with joy, and be led out with peace; the mountains and the hills shall break forth into singing before*

you, and all the trees of the field shall clap their hands (Isaiah 55:12).

Those who sow in tears shall reap in joy. He who continually goes forth weeping, bearing seed for sowing, shall doubtless come again with rejoicing, bringing his sheaves with him (Psalm 126:5-6).

How can we stay down when the Lord has given us such assurances to lift us up? Why should we starve ourselves in the beggar's corner when there is such a banquet at the King's table? Please pass the promises! Let's feast on! There are plenty more where these came from!

Daily Divine Encounters

God wants us to know Him through His daily presence. Most Christians tend to think of the presence of God as something they go to church to find. Well, I've got news for you. First, the presence of God is hard to find in many of our churches these days because He has been crowded out by all the meaningless and irrelevant "religious" things we do. That's why our churches are out of order. That's why we have lost our intimate relationship with God. That's why the house of God needs to be restored. Second, God is much too big to be confined inside any set of four walls. He is present and available anywhere, anytime. The reason so many of us fail to experience the peace, the power, and the presence of God is because we meet with Him only once a week. We need to learn to practice the presence of God in the everyday, routine activities of life. He wants us to know Him at home, at school, on the job, while washing the dishes or cutting the grass, while fixing the car or helping a neighbor.

It is important that we make plans to keep daily appointments with God. The more time we spend with God, the more we will know Him, and the more we know Him, the more we will love Him. The more we love Him, the more we will grow in Him. The more we grow in Him, the more power He will give us, the more peace He will give us, and the more joy He will give us. It is only by knowing God that we can enter into His purpose.

So much of the Church today is spiritually poverty-stricken because we have lost touch with the Lord. God wants to restore His house by taking us out of the gloom of the spiritual ghetto into the brightly sunlit courts of His royal palace and into a fresh awareness of our proper status as His royal heirs. He wants to see us claim our inheritance and realize our destiny as salt and light to the nations. In short, He wants to move us from poverty to purpose. Let's not be like C.S. Lewis's dwarves who could not see any greater destiny than a dirty stable. God has so much more for us than that. Once we reach out to Him in faith and let Him transform us and bring us back into intimate fellowship with Him, the *real* work can begin—*renovating the house!*

Endnote

1. R. Laird Harris, Gleason L. Archer, Jr., and Bruce K. Waltke, eds.; *Theological Wordbook of the Old Testament*, vol. 2; Chicago: Moody Press, 1980, "*para*," pp. 736-737.

CHAPTER EIGHT

Renovating the House

Have you ever watched those television programs that show the renovation of old houses? There's something fascinating about seeing a broken-down, unsightly, neglected house—sometimes little more than a stripped-out shell—transformed into a place of beauty, warm, cozy and inviting, fit to become a family *home*. Perhaps you have even renovated your own home. It's amazing how even just a little dressing up of the living room, kitchen, or bathroom can spark new life into a place. Something as simple as a fresh coat of paint can make a big difference.

To a certain extent, our attitudes are shaped by our surroundings. Most of us would behave differently in a shack than we would in a mansion. We all tend to adapt our behavior to the level of our environment. If we stay in the ghetto long enough, pretty soon we'll begin to think and act like the ghetto. This is one reason why it is so difficult for many people who live in negative circumstances—poverty, abusive relationships, multiple unwed pregnancies, etc.—to break the cycle. Their environment encourages the perpetuation of their condition. If they have no hope or expectation of anything better, they probably will not change.

At the same time, our surroundings often reflect our attitudes. A house with chipped and peeling paint, unmown grass, a door coming off its hinges, and trash and other junk strewn all over the yard conveys a very different image of its occupants than does a neat, trim house that is clean and in good repair. Appearances can be deceiving, of course, so we have to be careful not to judge. Yet, first impressions, whether right or wrong, are very difficult to change.

What impression does the world get when it looks at the Church today? In many cases, unfortunately, it sees us more as the neglected, junky house than as the clean, well-maintained one. Is it any wonder, then, that the world is not drawn to what we have to offer? What does the Church have to offer? That's the problem: Many of us just aren't sure anymore. Because we have lost touch with God, we have become confused about our message and have misplaced our map. How can we lead others when we don't know where we are going?

By and large, we who call ourselves Christians have become caretakers of a dilapidated house. I'm not talking about the physical appearance or condition of our worship facilities. Many of our church buildings are very beautiful and impressive structures. Unfortunately for many churches, a physically attractive building is all they have going for them. They are like the Pharisees that Jesus described as "whitewashed tombs which indeed appear beautiful outwardly, but inside are full of dead men's bones and all uncleanness" (Mt. 23:27b). The edifice looks nice on the outside, but there is no life on the inside.

No, the decrepit condition of the house of God is not readily visible to physical eyes. To see it we must learn to look through God's eyes. "For the Lord does not see as man sees; for man looks at the outward appearance, but the Lord looks at the heart" (1 Sam. 16:7b). A wasting spirit is creeping through much of the Church like wood rot through an old house. The first step in renovating a physical house is to determine exactly what needs to be done. Sometimes old, rotted wood must be torn out and replaced. The first step in renovating the house of God is to expose and clean out the rot of forgetfulness that is eating away at the framework.

The Rot of Forgetfulness

There is rampant in the Church of God today a spirit of forgetfulness that is wreaking havoc in the lives of believers. This spirit is divisive, deadly, and destructive—divisive because it separates us from the life-changing presence of God, deadly because it aborts the embryo of faith that God plants in the "heart-womb" of every believer, and destructive because it destroys our confidence in God's providential care.

Many of us have a tendency to forget all the things that the Lord brought us through in the past, particularly when times get tough in the present. Let's face it, if we're honest, every one of us can testify to some experience in our life when the only way we made it through was by the grace of God. Facing something that we could not deal with in our own strength, we turned to God, who brought us safely through to the other side. Yet, after all we have been through, and after all the times God has helped us, we still forget.

Our forgetfulness is not limited to the bad things in life; sometimes we forget about the blessings God has given. We pray for better circumstances and He provides us with a good education, a good job, a good income, a nice house, and a nice car. Then we forget. We get so busy enjoying these things that we forget who gave them to us. We may even begin to imagine that we got them solely because of our own efforts and intelligence. Either way, we get too busy for God: too busy to come to prayer meeting or worship, go to Bible study, help feed the hungry, or be part of a mentoring ministry. Everything we have and are is due to God's goodness, yet we forget.

The real problem with this spirit of forgetfulness is that it leads to denial. That's why so many of us do not live at the level of success and blessing that God wants for us. We spend our days denying by our actions and attitudes who God is and what He has done in our lives. It doesn't matter what we *say* we believe; our actions reveal what's really in our hearts. We may *say* we believe in prayer, yet deny its power by failing to pray. We may *say* we believe that nothing is impossible with God, yet deny it by failing to trust Him. We may *say* we believe that God will supply all our needs, yet deny it by depending only on our own resources. We deny God because we have forgotten what He has done for us.

Forgetfulness was a blight that plagued the Old Testament Israelites throughout their history. The Book of Deuteronomy, which relates Moses' instructions to the people shortly before they entered the promised land, is full of warnings against forgetting God.

> *Take heed to yourselves, lest you forget the covenant of the Lord your God which He made with you* (Deuteronomy 4:23a).

> *Then beware, lest you forget the Lord who brought you out of the land of Egypt, from the house of bondage* (Deuteronomy 6:12).

> *Beware that you do not forget the Lord your God by not keeping His commandments, His judgments, and His statutes which I command you today* (Deuteronomy 8:11).

> *Then it shall be, if you...forget the Lord your God...you shall surely perish* (Deuteronmy 8:19).

Despite these warnings, Israel repeatedly forgot the Lord, broke His covenant, and turned to idols, bringing His judgment upon them.

Because of Jacob's encounters with God there, Bethel became a sacred place to the Israelites, which they didn't forget. Even after 400 years in Egypt and 40 years in the wilderness, when the Israelites finally entered the promised land, Bethel remained a sacred and special place, representing for them the presence and voice of God. When the people forgot God, however, Bethel became polluted. As we saw in Chapter One, beginning with the reign of Jeroboam, the first king of the southern kingdom of Judah, Bethel became a site for idolatrous worship. By the time of King Josiah centuries later, pagan worship was well established at Bethel and at other places in the land, and the people as a whole had forgotten God. They had forgotten what God had done for them, they had forgotten His Law, and they had forgotten His house. The splendid temple that Solomon had built had fallen into disrepair. Josiah, who had a heart for God, undertook to renovate the temple. "In the eighteenth year of his reign, when he had purged the land and the temple, he sent Shaphan the son of Azaliah, Maaseiah the governor of the city, and Joah the son of Joahaz the recorder, to repair the house of the Lord his God" (2 Chron. 34:8). Josiah's work in this regard provides us with a platform for understanding how to renovate the house of God today. It begins with *remembrance*.

Remember Therefore From Where You Have Fallen

The antidote to the poison of forgetfulness is the elixir of remembrance. Remembering what God has done for us and what He expects of us is the first step toward spiritual recovery. Another step is remembering our sins that have caused us to turn away from Him. The Holy Spirit brings all of these things to our minds. We are then responsible before God as to how we respond.

Josiah was eight years old when he became king, and when he was 16, he began to seek the Lord. At the age of 20, he initiated spiritual reforms in the land and "began to purge Judah and Jerusalem of the high places, the wooden images, the carved images, and the molded images" (2 Chron. 34:3b). Six years later, he began repairs on the temple. Early in this process, while the temple was being cleaned, "Hilkiah the priest found the Book of the Law of the Lord given by Moses" (2 Chron. 34:14b). It was then that things *really* kicked into high gear.

> Then Shaphan the scribe told the king, saying, "Hilkiah the priest has given me a book." And Shaphan read it before the king. Thus it happened, when the king heard the words of the Law, that he tore his clothes. Then the king commanded Hilkiah, Ahikam the son of Shaphan, Abdon the son of Micah, Shaphan the scribe, and Asaiah a servant of the king, saying,

> *"Go, inquire of the Lord for me, and for those who are left in Israel and Judah, concerning the words of the book that is found; for great is the wrath of the Lord that is poured out on us, because our fathers have not kept the word of the Lord, to do according to all that is written in this book"* (2 Chronicles 34:18-21).

For Josiah, the Book of the Law became a book of remembrance. As it was read in his hearing, Josiah remembered the commandments and mighty acts of God in the past, and was cut to the heart over the people's subsequent unfaithfulness and disobedience. Remembrance resulted in repentance.

Just as the scriptural warnings against forgetting are many, the call to remember is great.

> *And Moses said to the people: "Remember this day in which you went out of Egypt, out of the house of bondage; for by strength of hand the Lord brought you out of this place...* (Exodus 13:3).

> *And you shall remember the Lord your God, for it is He who gives you power to get wealth, that He may establish His covenant which He swore to your fathers, as it is this day* (Deuteronomy 8:18).

> *I will remember the works of the Lord; surely I will remember Your wonders of old* (Psalm 77:11).

> *Remember His marvelous works which He has done, His wonders, and the judgments of His mouth* (Psalm 105:5).

> *Remember therefore from where you have fallen; repent and do the first works* (Revelation 2:5a).

> *Remember therefore how you have received and heard; hold fast and repent* (Revelation 3:3a).

It's time to take a trip down memory lane. If our house is going to be renovated, we must remember who we once were before we knew the Lord, and where He has brought us since then. We should never get so cute, so educated, or so uppity and puffed-up that we don't remember where we came from. Remembering may be painful as the Spirit of God convicts us of our rebellion, forgetfulness, disobedience, and worldliness. When those kinds of memories surface, the only appropriate response is repentance. We can't expect to see our house restored while at the same time holding on to the very things that brought the house down in the first place.

When we remember what God has done for us, when we remember what God requires, when we remember from where we have fallen and repent, a door is opened for God to make a way to lead us back. Repentance means turning around and going in the opposite direction from before. Remembrance is the first step, but alone it is not enough. The next step in renovating our spiritual house is to *return*.

Return to Me

When Josiah was reminded of the demands of God's Law, the people's failure to obey God, and the wrath of God that awaited them, he sent a party of trusted advisors to "inquire of the Lord." These men sought out Hulda, a prophetess, who gave them a message from the Lord to pass on to the king. Hulda's prophecy contained both good news and bad news. The bad news was that the sins of the people were so great that nothing—not even the wholesale repentance of the nation—could now turn away the judgment that God had pronounced. It was inescapable. The good news was that because the king had a tender heart, and had humbled himself and sought the Lord, God's judgment on the nation would be withheld until after Josiah's death. The king's righteousness and humility had bought a reprieve for the people.

This message from God galvanized the young king into even greater efforts at reform. Josiah became even more deeply committed to returning the nation of Judah to God's ways.

Then the king sent and gathered all the elders of Judah and Jerusalem. The king went up to the house of the Lord, with all the men of Judah and the inhabitants of Jerusalem; the priests and the Levites, and all the people, great and small. And he read in their hearing all the words of the Book of the Covenant which had been found in the house of the Lord. Then the king stood in his place and made a covenant before the Lord, to follow the Lord, and to keep His commandments and His testimonies and His statutes with all his heart and all his soul, to perform the words of the covenant that were written in this book. And he made all who were present in Jerusalem and Benjamin take a stand. So the inhabitants of Jerusalem did according to the covenant of God, the God of their fathers (2 Chronicles 34:29-32).

By example and decree, Josiah led the people of Judah to return to the Lord, to repent and to reaffirm their commitment to "the covenant of God, the God of their fathers." Even though eventual judgment was inevitable, Josiah recognized that the people would be much better off facing that judgment in a restored condition than in a rebellious state. Judgment or not, the *right* place to be was on the Lord's side.

The theme of returning to God runs throughout the Scriptures. From the fall of man in the opening chapters of Genesis to the "new heaven" and "new earth" in the closing chapters of Revelation, the Bible reveals a God who pursues the return of sinners to Him in repentance and faith. One of the sweetest admonitions in Scripture is found in the simple words, "Return to Me."

I have blotted out, like a thick cloud, your transgressions, and like a cloud, your sins. Return to Me, for I have redeemed you (Isaiah 44:22).

"If you will return, O Israel," says the Lord, "return to Me; and if you will put away your abominations out of My sight, then you shall not be moved" (Jeremiah 4:1).

Then I will give them a heart to know Me, that I am the Lord; and they shall be My people, and I will be their God, for they shall return to Me with their whole heart (Jeremiah 24:7).

"Return to Me, and I will return to you," says the Lord of hosts (Malachi 3:7b).

No matter who we are or where we have been, the Lord is calling us to return to Him. Why is it that in the midst of our trials and our troubles, our hardships and our difficulties, when Christ could turn us around and lead us out, that so often He is the *last* person we turn to? We get beaten up by life so much of the time because we fail to learn the lesson God is trying to teach us: *Return to Me.* When we fail to learn from our problems, we often repeat those problems, going through the same old stuff time after time. When are we going to wake up? Sometimes the Lord just keeps us in the same place until we learn to trust Him and return to Him. When we do return to Him and take our problems to Him, we will discover that He is with us in the midst of our difficulties, waiting to bring us out. However, before He can help us, we must return to Him.

Once we have returned to the Lord and gotten our faces pointed in the right direction again, it is time for the next step in the renovation of our house: *rebuilding*.

Rebuilding the Ruins

Any successful renovation requires a plan or a pattern for the builders or restorers to follow. Whether it is a written description or a blueprint, the plan gives guidance for accomplishing the work. Whenever we return to the Lord, we are indicating our desire for our lives and our churches to be restored to their original condition, conforming to God's master plan, as well as our willingness to submit to whatever reconstruction is deemed necessary by the Carpenter and Master Builder. This may involve first ripping out and discarding the old, rotten, corrupt, polluted "junk" from the world before the clean, fresh, and new things of the Spirit can be applied.

Josiah's message from the Lord inspired him to greater devotion to God and stronger determination to renovate the temple and cleanse the land from all semblances of idolatry and other false religious practices.

111

And the king commanded Hilkiah the high priest, the priests of the second order, and the doorkeepers, to bring out of the temple of the Lord all the articles that were made for Baal, for Asherah, and for all the host of heaven; and he burned them outside Jerusalem in the fields of Kidron, and carried their ashes to Bethel. Then he removed the idolatrous priests whom the kings of Judah had ordained to burn incense on the high places in the cities of Judah and in the places all around Jerusalem, and those who burned incense to Baal, to the sun, to the moon, to the constellations, and to all the host of heaven. And he brought out the wooden image from the house of the Lord, to the Brook Kidron outside Jerusalem, burned it at the Brook Kidron and ground it to ashes, and threw its ashes on the graves of the common people. Then he tore down the ritual booths of the perverted persons that were in the house of the Lord, where the women wove hangings for the wooden image (2 Kings 23:4-7).

Pagan idols and immoral worship practices such as prostitution and sexual perversion had invaded even the temple of God! Josiah rooted it all out. He burned or smashed the idols and all their trappings, deposed and executed the idolatrous priests, and defiled and destroyed pagan worship sites and high places throughout the land. Josiah had a burning fever to rebuild the temple, the people, and the land according to God's master plan as revealed in the Book of the Covenant, which Shaphan the scribe had read to him.

After times of rebellion and departure, repentance and return, comes the time to rebuild. The Word of God acknowledges this cycle in the life of God's people and encourages the process.

For we were slaves. Yet our God did not forsake us in our bondage; but He extended mercy to us in the sight of the kings of Persia, to revive us, to repair the house of our God, to rebuild its ruins, and to give us a wall in Judah and Jerusalem (Ezra 9:9).

And they shall rebuild the old ruins, they shall raise up the former desolations, and they shall repair the ruined cities, the desolations of many generations (Isaiah 61:4).

And I will cause the captives of Judah and the captives of Israel to return, and will rebuild those places as at the first (Jeremiah 33:7).

On that day I will raise up the tabernacle of David, which has fallen down, and repair its damages; I will raise up its ruins, and rebuild it as in the days of old (Amos 9:11).

When we give God a free hand to rebuild and renovate our house, He will walk through from attic to basement stripping away everything that is not of Him, purging and cleansing us of every taint and stain of the world. Simply covering over the blemishes with new plaster or fresh paint won't do; He wants them *out!* Our churches are filled with people who display outwardly a bright and shining, devout and pious demeanor which is in reality a shroud concealing sin, corruption, and death. Like many of the churches they attend, these folks are little more than "whitewashed tombs."

Before pointing our finger at others, however, we would do well to look deep into our own hearts. If the Master Builder surveyed your house or mine to determine what renovation is needed, what would He find? Be warned! When He goes to work on us, He will be merciless in ripping out every "work" of the flesh: "...adultery, fornication, uncleanness, lewdness, idolatry, sorcery, hatred, contentions, jealousies, outbursts of wrath, selfish ambitions, dissensions, heresies, envy, murders, drunkenness, revelries, and the like" (Gal. 5:19-21a). Let them go! We don't need them, because in their place He will build in us character, courage, conviction, commitment, and integrity, as well as the fruit of the Spirit: "...love, joy, peace, longsuffering, kindness, goodness, faithfulness, gentleness, [and] self-control" (Gal. 5:22-23a). Such reconstruction as this will hurt for awhile, but the benefits far outweigh the cost. The long-term gain is worth the short-term pain.

Are you ready and willing to let the Lord, the Chief Carpenter, do whatever He needs to do in your heart and life in order to rebuild you according to His original blueprint? If so, why don't you tell Him right now!

Renew Our Days

After rebuilding comes renewal. Renovation is complete and the house has a new lease on life, purpose, and usefulness. It is now better fitted for fulfilling its function—providing shelter, warmth, and protection, as well as a nurturing environment for growth. If our spiritual house is out of order, all these functions are out of order as well, and everyone in the house suffers. The cold winds of false doctrines, deceit, and worldliness whistle through the cracks in the walls of our faith and understanding, leaving us shivering in their wake. Lacking a coherent sense of direction, dissension and division break out within the family. When the house has been rebuilt and renewed, however, the wayward winds are shut out, the Master is present to manage the affairs of His house, and all is well.

Once Josiah completed the renovation of the temple and the cleansing of the land, he led the people in a recommitment to their covenant with God which brought renewal to the nation.

Now Josiah kept a Passover to the Lord in Jerusalem, and they slaughtered the Passover lambs on the fourteenth day of the first month. And he set the priests in their duties and encouraged them for the service of the house of the Lord. Then he said to the Levites who taught all Israel, who were holy to the Lord: "Put the holy ark in the house which Solomon the son of David, king of Israel, built. It shall no longer be a burden on your shoulders. Now serve the Lord your God and His people Israel....So slaughter the Passover offerings, consecrate yourselves, and prepare them for your brethren, that they may do according to the word of the Lord by the hand of Moses." Then Josiah gave the lay people lambs and young goats from the flock, all for Passover offerings for all who were present, to the number of thirty thousand, as well as three thousand cattle; these were from the king's possessions....And the children of Israel who were present kept the Passover at that time, and the Feast of Unleavened Bread for seven days. There had been no Passover kept in Israel like that since the days of Samuel the prophet; and none of the kings of Israel had kept such a Passover as Josiah kept, with the priests and the Levites, all Judah and Israel who were present, and the inhabitants of Jerusalem (2 Chronicles 35:1-3,6-7,17-18).

The young king, the priests, and the people, all praising and worshiping God with one heart and voice—my, what a glorious celebration it must have been! After the hot, dry wind of sin, separation, and confusion came the cool, refreshing breeze of reconciliation and the presence of God. Despite the pronouncement of certain judgment, God still reached out to His children. Through the humble heart of a godly king, the Lord had called His people to renewal.

God still calls His people to renewal. It is a recurring theme throughout Scripture.

Create in me a clean heart, O God, and renew a steadfast spirit within me (Psalm 51:10).

Turn us back to You, O Lord, and we will be restored; renew our days as of old (Lamentations 5:21).

Therefore we do not lose heart. Even though our outward man is perishing, yet the inward man is being renewed day by day (2 Corinthians 4:16).

That you put off, concerning your former conduct, the old man which grows corrupt according to the deceitful lusts, and be renewed in the spirit of your mind, and that you put on the new man which was created according to God, in true righteousness and holiness (Ephesians 4:22-24).

Repent therefore and be converted, that your sins may be blotted out, so that times of refreshing may come from the presence of the Lord (Acts 3:19).

When we do our part, the Lord will do His. When we respond to His call to remember and return, He will rebuild and renew us.

To renew simply means to make new again. The restoration of our spiritual house is not complete until renewal comes. Just as God gave Jacob a new nature when He changed his name to Israel, He must give each of us a new nature as well. Otherwise, we would not know how to handle His blessings. Besides, the new nature in Christ is essential for our salvation. We have no hope of Heaven without it. The renovation process is necessary because we have to let our old nature die so our new nature, the Christ-nature in us, can arise. "Therefore, if anyone is in Christ, he is a new creation; old things have passed away; behold, all things have become new" (2 Cor. 5:17).

A restored Church is a renewed Church, and a renewed Church is ready to take on the world. We have been through so much, and God has brought us so far, that there are some things we simply won't stand for anymore. Gone are the days of defeat and negativism. *Christ has made all things new!* Gone are the days of intimidation in the face of a hostile culture. *Christ has made all things new!* Gone are the days of silence, apology, and defensiveness in the face of godless and humanistic philosophies. *Christ has made all things new!* Gone are the days of retreat before a morally and spiritually indifferent society. *Christ has made all things new!* Gone are the days of surrender before the principalities, powers of the air, and rulers of the darkness. *Christ has made all things new!*

A renewed Church is a victorious Church, a Church that functions fully in *every dimension.*

CHAPTER NINE

The Seven Habits of Highly Effective Churches

America on the threshold of a new millennium is a selfish, pleasure-seeking, entertainment-obsessed society. Ours is the first truly "high-tech" generation in history. Television's pervasive influence is felt in virtually every home. Cable and network news organizations bring world events into our living rooms as they happen. Personal satellite dishes make hundreds of channels and thousands of programs available at the push of a button. Fiber optic networks and cellular phones with signals bounced off special satellites keep us connected globally. A network of other satellites makes it possible for a person using a handheld global positioning indicator to identify his exact location anywhere on the earth. Personal computers, the Internet, and the Worldwide Web make communication, knowledge, information, business transactions, and entertainment immediately available to a degree never before imagined. In the social and cultural senses, technology truly has shrunken our world.

There is a great paradox here. Even as our ability for greater social interaction grows, our social isolation increases. In many ways life is becoming more impersonal every day. The very technology

117

that has made intimate social interaction possible has also made it unnecessary. Today we can carry on virtually every aspect of our lives without ever leaving our homes or having to see or talk to another person face-to-face. This contributes to a growing sense of emptiness and pointlessness in life that already plagues millions of Americans. We are in danger of becoming as flat and two-dimensional as the images on our television and computer screens.

We try to cope with this void in our hearts in many different ways. Some people simply wander through life from day to day without goal, ambition, or hope. Others try to fill the void with things they think will bring them pleasure, release, or escape: drugs, alcohol, sex, pornography, gambling, deliberate risk-taking and daredevil behavior, "extreme" sports, etc. In recent years there has been an upsurge in people's interest in "spirituality," ranging from the occult to New Age philosophies to religious cults. Even this spiritual interest is primarily selfish, however, focusing on meeting personal needs and gratifying personal desires.

Our appetite for entertainment is insatiable. So much of what we do centers around what we think will interest us, amuse us, benefit us, or divert us for a time from the pain and emptiness of life. The thought uppermost in our selfish, greedy minds is "What's in this for *me*? How will this help *me* get ahead?"

One reason why so many churches today are out of order and ineffective in reaching their communities is because this same entertainment mindset has infected the hearts and attitudes of the worshipers. For many church members, Sunday morning worship is the "entertainment hour" rather than an appointed time to meet with and honor God. Churches that have been restored and renewed, however, have their hearts and focus in the right place where worship is concerned. These churches practice what we could call the "seven habits of highly effective churches": the *worship* of God, the *Word* of God, the *will* of God, the *work* of God, the *witness* to God, the *wealth* of God, and the *warfare* of God. Worship is first because it is the most essential, yet least understood and practiced habit of all. It is the core around which everything else is built.

In Spirit and in Truth?

Jesus told the Samaritan woman at the well, "God is Spirit, and those who worship Him must worship in spirit and truth" (Jn. 4:24). This verse defines a kind of worship that is a far cry from what many—perhaps most—churches experience on Sunday mornings. Most of what we call "worship," whether preaching or singing, is really just entertainment designed to make the flesh feel good. That's what many churchgoers are looking for. They run from church to church hunting the elusive "warm fuzzy." As long as the music of the choir or soloist sends a tingle up their spines, or as long as the preacher's sermon lifts them up and makes them feel good about themselves, they're fine. They hang around as long as it lasts. Sooner or later, however, something will happen to make them feel uncomfortable again, and off they'll go to another place, looking for a fresh dose of "Dr. Feel-Good."

No church likes to lose members, so it is easy for pastors and other leadership to give in to the temptation to appeal to the flesh in order to keep people coming. Instead of preaching sermons that will convict, challenge, and change worshipers, pastors opt for messages that will stroke egos, entertain, and make minimal demands on those listening. This is why we don't see revival in our cities or across our land. We spend our "worship" time entertaining the flesh instead of seeking the face of God.

God has so much more for us than that. He has promised in His Word that those who diligently seek Him will find Him (see Jer. 29:13). Like the Canaanite woman who was satisfied with the crumbs from Jesus' table (see Mt. 15:22-28), many of us come to church Sunday after Sunday content to get just the "leftovers" of God's glory. As long as we are satisfied to feed our flesh with crumbs, we will miss out on the feast that God has prepared for us. Moving beyond the entertainment of the flesh into obedience to God and seeking His face will lead us to His banquet table. Learning how to worship "in spirit and truth" is the road to the "more" of God. Along that road lie three "way stations" that take us deeper into the truth and presence of God: thanksgiving, praise, and holiness.

In Everything Give Thanks

Giving thanks is the simplest and easiest way to worship. Anybody can do it because everybody has something to be thankful for. All we have to do is think a little bit and remember what God has done for us and how He takes care of us. God gives us life, health, food, and drink to nourish us, clothing for our bodies, shoes for our feet, a roof over our heads to protect and shelter us from the weather, and jobs so we can earn money to pay our bills and support our families. God's Word promises that He will care for those who put their trust in Him. "The steps of a good man are ordered by the Lord, and He delights in his way. Though he fall, he shall not be utterly cast down; for the Lord upholds him with His hand. I have been young, and now am old; yet I have not seen the righteous forsaken, nor his descendants begging bread" (Ps. 37:23-25). How should we respond to such a promise as this? At the most basic level, we should give thanks to God.

Thanksgiving is a matter of faith, but it is also a command from the Lord. "Oh, give thanks to the Lord, for He is good! For His mercy endures forever" (Ps. 107:1). "In everything give thanks; for this is the will of God in Christ Jesus for you" (1 Thess. 5:18). "And whatever you do in word or deed, do all in the name of the Lord Jesus, giving thanks to God the Father through Him" (Col. 3:17). Because of God's bountiful goodness to us, it should be easy to obey this command. Yet, there are some folks who come to church and never thank God for anything. Instead, they act as if they think God *owes* them something, as if He is *obligated* to provide them with that house, that car, that job, or that education.

An unthankful spirit is a canker which, left unchecked, will quickly infect and corrupt the whole body. It will turn your heart to stone and your blood to ice. It will sear your soul, leaving it arid, barren, bitter, and lifeless. It will destroy your peace, disrupt your fellowship with God and eat you away inside like a cancer. In Second

Timothy 3:2, the apostle Paul lists unthankfulness as one of the characteristics of enemies of God. It is *impossible* to have an unthankful heart and be right with God. It is *impossible* to have an unthankful spirit and enter into true worship.

The benefits of a thankful spirit are many. Thankfulness is a characteristic of God's peace. "And let the peace of God rule in your hearts, to which also you were called in one body; and be thankful" (Col. 3:15). Thankfulness is an antidote for anxiety. "Be anxious for nothing, but in everything by prayer and supplication, with thanksgiving, let your requests be made known to God" (Phil. 4:6). Thankfulness is healthy for body and mind. "A merry heart does good, like medicine, but a broken spirit dries the bones" (Prov. 17:22). Thankfulness is a close companion of joy. "Let us come before His presence with thanksgiving; let us shout joyfully to Him with psalms" (Ps. 95:2). Thankfulness ushers us into the courts of the Lord. "Enter into His gates with thanksgiving, and into His courts with praise. Be thankful to Him, and bless His name" (Ps. 100:4).

Thanksgiving is the most basic level of worship. As believers we are all called and commanded to give thanks to the Lord. In the school of worship, thanksgiving is the *primer*, the basic language skills book that prepares us for the next level. Thanksgiving acknowledges God for what He has *done*. The next level or dimension of worship is *praise*, which acknowledges God simply for who He *is*.

A Sacrifice of Praise

Praise and thanksgiving are very closely related; in fact, in the minds of many the terms are almost interchangeable. The distinction lies in that while thanksgiving exalts God for what He has done for us or for others, praise lifts God up because of who He is. Thanksgiving exalts the *deeds* of God; praise exalts the *Person* of God—His name, His nature, and His character. We thank God for what He has done for us; we praise God simply because He is God, and as Creator and King of the universe, is worthy and deserving of our praise.

121

Praise brings us closer to the pure light of God's glory because it lifts us out of ourselves. Thanksgiving is always "selfish" to a certain degree because we are focusing on what God has done for *us* and thanking Him for it. Pure praise, on the other hand, has nothing selfish in it; praise is centered totally on God. This is why praise could be considered a "higher" level of worship than thanksgiving. When we praise God, we lose ourselves in the brightness of His glory and the beauty of His holiness. When we get ourselves out of the way in praise, we are no longer concerned about how we look to other people or what they think about us. We stop worrying about our pride, our position, or our dignity. Our attention, our thoughts, our whole being are concentrated on our Lord in all His splendor and beauty.

Like thanksgiving, praise is commanded in the Scripture. "Praise the Lord! I will praise the Lord with my whole heart, in the assembly of the upright and in the congregation" (Ps. 111:1). "Praise the Lord! Blessed is the man who fears the Lord, who delights greatly in His commandments" (Ps. 112:1). "Praise the Lord! Praise, O servants of the Lord, praise the name of the Lord!" (Ps. 113:1) "Praise the Lord! For it is good to sing praises to our God; for it is pleasant, and praise is beautiful" (Ps. 147:1). "Praise the Lord! Praise God in His sanctuary; praise Him in His mighty firmament!...Let everything that has breath praise the Lord. Praise the Lord!" (Ps. 150:1,6) "Therefore by Him let us continually offer the sacrifice of praise to God, that is, the fruit of our lips, giving thanks to His name" (Heb. 13:15).

"Let everything that has breath praise the Lord." That means you, me, all of us. It doesn't matter how old you are or how young you are. It makes no difference whether you can speak eloquently or whether you stutter with every word. Education doesn't matter; neither does job nor position. We are to praise God when we have money and when we don't. We are to praise Him when we are healthy and when we are sick. We are to praise God during good times and bad. Whatever our circumstance or situation, we are to praise the Lord. Praise has an infectious quality about it. Even when we don't feel like praising the Lord, if we obey His command to praise Him with our lips, pretty soon it spreads to our minds and hearts. Before long, we can't even remember that we weren't in the mood for praise.

Praise lifts us to a higher plane of worship and prepares us to draw near to the Lord "in the beauty of holiness." Nothing that is corrupt or of the flesh can enter the holy presence of God, so it must be stripped away and laid aside. Our flesh must be crucified with Christ before we can approach His holiness. This is part of what is meant by offering a "sacrifice of praise."

In the Beauty of Holiness

The psalmist wrote, "Worship the Lord in the beauty of holiness" (Ps. 29:2b). Effective churches practice the habit of intimate, life-changing worship of God in His holiness. This includes not only thanksgiving and praise but also entering into the "Most Holy Place" of God's divine presence. Psalm 22:3 says, "But You are holy, enthroned in the praises of Israel." This means that when the praises go up, the blessings come down; when the praises ascend, the Presence descends.

Only that which is holy—absolutely pure—can abide in the presence of a holy God. If we want to move into the highest plane of worship in the presence of that holiness, we must *be* holy and *live* holy. We must deny the flesh with its sin and corruption and take up the righteousness of Christ. The apostle Paul described it this way: "Knowing this, that our old man was crucified with Him, that the body of sin might be done away with, that we should no longer be slaves of sin" (Rom. 6:6). In his letter to the Ephesians, Paul admonished the church to "put off, concerning your former conduct, the old man which grows corrupt according to the deceitful lusts, and be renewed in the spirit of your mind, and that you put on the new man which was created according to God, in true righteousness and holiness" (Eph. 4:22-24). Peter also stressed the importance of holy living. "But as He who called you is holy, you also be holy in all your conduct, because it is written, 'Be holy, for I am holy' " (1 Pet. 1:15-16). The secret to moving from fleshly entertainment to full-fledged, empowered worship is to crucify the flesh.

A woman I know and love who is like a mother to me once told me something that changed my entire attitude toward worship. She said, "Frank, the Lord's presence is everything." The goal of worship is to enter into the presence of God. Holiness is the requirement. Christ has made us holy by His death on the cross for our sins, but we have the responsibility to live holy. Learning to live holy is neither quick nor easy. It requires commitment, determination, and effort. We have to decide before God that we are going to stop thinking like the world, living like the world, and letting the world determine our values and attitudes. God's standards must become our standards, His thoughts our thoughts, and His ways our ways. After all, worship is not about us—it's about God. It's not about how we look or sound or feel, or about doing our own thing. Worship means being obedient to what God says to us. *Effective churches worship the living God.*

Sharper Than Any Two-edged Sword

The second habit of highly effective churches is an absolute commitment to the Word of God: studying it, teaching it, preaching it, and living it. Some of you might ask, "Frank, why did you put worship ahead of the Word? Shouldn't the Bible be central in everything we do?" In reality, worship and the Word go together, but I listed worship first because it is so important that we understand the place of intimacy and the presence of God. Emphasizing the Word *over* worship leads easily to legalism, where you have the letter of the law but not the intimacy that only worship can provide. This was the problem of the scribes and Pharisees in Jesus' day. Although they were experts in the law and knew the Scriptures better than anyone else in the land, Jesus said to them, "You search the Scriptures, for in them you think you have eternal life; and these are they which testify of Me. But you are not willing to come to Me that you may have life" (Jn. 5:39-40). The scribes and Pharisees knew the Scriptures, but they did not know the God who wrote them!

Worship without the Word is just as dangerous, because we have no theological and doctrinal grounding to provide a standard by which to interpret and understand our experiences. Worship brings us into the presence of the glory of God while the Word of God gives us structure and guidance in every area of our lives. Paul wrote to Timothy, "All Scripture is given by inspiration of God, and is profitable for doctrine, for reproof, for correction, for instruction in righteousness, that the man of God may be complete, thoroughly equipped for every good work" (2 Tim. 3:16-17). Intimacy with God means *knowing* God. We come to know God as we experience His presence in worship, as He speaks to us through His Word, and as the Holy Spirit who dwells within us interprets God's Word for us so we can understand it.

Effective churches give a premium place to dynamic worship in spirit and truth. They also center their worship and ministry around the bold, confident, unapologetic preaching and teaching of the Word of God. God's Word is part of the "whole armor of God" that Paul describes in the sixth chapter of Ephesians: "And take the helmet of salvation, and the sword of the Spirit, which is the word of God" (Eph. 6:17). The writer of Hebrews said, "For the word of God is living and powerful, and sharper than any two-edged sword, piercing even to the division of soul and spirit, and of joints and marrow, and is a discerner of the thoughts and intents of the heart" (Heb. 4:12). The dynamic presence of God and the explosive power of His Word arm a church with unassailable authority and unwavering courage to storm the gates of hell and set the captives free. *Effective churches preach the Word of God.*

Not My Will, but Yours Be Done

The third habit of highly effective churches is discerning and doing the *will* of God. As we learn to worship God in Spirit and truth, and as we become grounded in the Word of God, out of that intimacy we become sensitive to the will of God. The focus of our attention turns to what He wants, not what we want. Jesus Himself set the example for us in the garden of Gethsemane the night before His crucifixion when He said, "Father, if it is Your will, take this cup away from Me; nevertheless not My will, but Yours, be done" (Lk. 22:42). Jesus was given over completely to doing the will and purpose of His Father. "Most assuredly, I say to you, the Son can do nothing of Himself, but what He sees the Father do; for whatever He does, the Son also does in like manner....I can of Myself do nothing. As I hear, I judge; and My judgment is righteous, because I do not seek My own will but the will of the Father who sent Me" (Jn. 5:19b,30).

We who claim to follow Jesus must seek to do as He did. If Jesus sought only the will of the Father, how much more then should we? It is only in seeking and doing the will of God that we find and fulfill our purpose, whether as individual believers or as a church. When we are out of order and out of fellowship with God, it is impossible to know and do His will because we are already out of His will!

How do we learn God's will? It all goes back to the element of sacrifice. "I beseech you therefore, brethren, by the mercies of God, that you present your bodies a living sacrifice, holy, acceptable to God, which is your reasonable service. And do not be conformed to this world, but be transformed by the renewing of your mind, that you may prove what is that good and acceptable and perfect will of God" (Rom. 12:1-2). Jesus sacrificed His life, not just on the cross, but by living every moment in complete surrender to His Father. Likewise, we come to know the will of God by seeking in humility and faith to follow Him every moment, always yielding our will to His control. Once we learn to quiet the proud posturing of our own will, we can hear the voice of God, and when we can hear His voice, He will reveal His will. *Effective churches obey the will of God.*

To the Work

Once we know the will of God, we are prepared to do the *work* of God. The fourth habit of highly effective churches is that they do the work God has given them to do and dispense with the rest. If a church ceases to do the work of God, it ceases to be a true church. There are many, many churches that are very busy with all sorts of programs, ministries, activities, and yet are spinning their wheels because they are not doing the work God gave them to do.

What is the work of God that we are to do? Specific assignments will vary from church to church and city to city as God makes known to each one where He is working and what He is doing in each place. However, the Scriptures reveal several key activities that are always the work of God at any time and any place. Consider these verses:

> *Jesus said to them, "My food is to do the will of Him who sent Me, and to finish His work. Do you not say, 'There are still four months and then comes the harvest'? Behold, I say to you, lift up your eyes and look at the fields, for they are already white for harvest! And he who reaps receives wages, and gathers fruit for eternal life, that both he who sows and he who reaps may rejoice together"* (John 4:34-36).

> *Now all things are of God, who has reconciled us to Himself through Jesus Christ, and has given us the ministry of reconciliation, that is, that God was in Christ reconciling the world to Himself, not imputing their trespasses to them, and has committed to us the word of reconciliation* (2 Corinthians 5:18-19).

> *Then they said to Him, "What shall we do, that we may work the works of God?" Jesus answered and said to them, "This is the work of God, that you believe in Him whom He sent"* (John 6:28-29).

> *"I have glorified You on the earth. I have finished the work which You have given Me to do"* (John 17:4).

> *And He said to them, "Go into all the world and preach the gospel to every creature* (Mark 16:15).

As we worship, preach the Word and search out the will of God, He renews our vision, which inspires us to be about His work. We strive to make that vision a reality as we labor to rebuild broken families, restore broken cities, feed the hungry, shelter the homeless, and take the message of Christ to the nations. There is an old gospel hymn by Fanny J. Crosby that expresses so well what it means to do the work of God.

> To the work! To the work! We are servants of God,
> Let us follow the path that our Master has trod;
> With the balm of His counsel our strength to renew,
> Let us do with our might what our hands find to do.
> To the work! To the work! Let the hungry be fed;
> To the fountain of life let the weary be led;
> In the cross and its banner our glory shall be,
> While we herald the tidings, "Salvation is free!"
> Toiling on, toiling on, toiling on, toiling on,
> Let us hope and trust, let us watch and pray,
> And labor till the Master comes.

Effective churches carry on the work of God.

You Shall Be Witnesses

The fifth habit of highly effective churches is that they witness to God before the world. They proclaim to the world the greatness, the love, the mercy, the grace, and the mighty works of God. This is a true and effective witness because it is based not on words alone, but also on actions. We become effective witnesses because we are witnessing through our work. Our work is rooted prayerfully in the will of God, which we obey as revealed in the Word of God and confirmed to us in our worship of God. Effective witness involves both words and actions. James said, "Thus also faith by itself, if it does not have works, is dead. But someone will say, 'You have faith, and I have works.' Show me your faith without your works, and I will show you my faith by my works....You see then that a man is justified by works, and not by faith only" (Jas. 2:17-18,24). This does not mean that we are saved by our good works, but that our good works verify or give proof of the faith that we profess with our lips.

One of the last issues Jesus addressed with His disciples before He ascended to the Father was their witness before the world. "Go therefore and make disciples of all the nations, baptizing them in the name of the Father and of the Son and of the Holy Spirit, teaching them to observe all things that I have commanded you" (Mt. 28:19-20a). In the Greek, the imperative command *go* is in a tense that indicates continuing action; it could be translated, "as you go." *As we go* about the normal affairs of life, day by day and moment by moment, we are to make disciples as we witness through our words, our actions, and our lifestyle.

The last recorded words of Jesus before His ascension also dealt with this same subject. "But you shall receive power when the Holy Spirit has come upon you; and you shall be witnesses to Me in Jerusalem, and in all Judea and Samaria, and to the end of the earth" (Acts 1:8). The basic Greek word for "witnesses" is *martus*, from which the English word *martyr* comes. So, a true and effective witness is that which is lived out—even to the death if necessary—rather than simply talked about.

Being a witness does not always mean knocking on doors, necessarily, but it does mean learning to live out in everyday life the truth of Jesus' words when He said:

> *You are the salt of the earth; but if the salt loses its flavor, how shall it be seasoned? It is then good for nothing but to be thrown out and trampled underfoot by men. You are the light of the world. A city that is set on a hill cannot be hidden. Nor do they light a lamp and put it under a basket, but on a lampstand, and it gives light to all who are in the house. Let your light so shine before men, that they may see your good works and glorify your Father in heaven* (Matthew 5:13-16).

We are the salt of the earth and the light of the world. The witness of both our *words* and our *works* should point people to the Father. *Effective churches witness to God.*

Treasures in Heaven

As effective churches grow through worship, are grounded in the Word, obey the will of God by carrying out His work and witnessing to Him before the world, they learn to practice a sixth habit: *enjoying the wealth of God.*

I'm not talking about material prosperity here—that may or may not come—but *spiritual* wealth. Jesus said, "Do not lay up for yourselves treasures on earth, where moth and rust destroy and where thieves break in and steal; but lay up for yourselves treasures in heaven, where neither moth nor rust destroys and where thieves do not break in and steal. For where your treasure is, there your heart will be also" (Mt. 6:19-21).

What kind of treasures are we talking about here? How about the treasure of a healthy spirit or the riches of joy that come from helping someone else in Jesus' name? What about the priceless gift of knowing that our sins have been forgiven and that we have eternal life in Jesus Christ our Lord? Don't forget the precious jewel of intimacy with God! What could be worth more than God's presence with us through bad times as well as good? Just ask someone who has walked through the valley of the shadow of death and found Christ right there walking alongside him!

We may never be millionaires, but if we honor and follow the principles about money and material things that God has set out in His Word, He will cause us to prosper. This means that if we are faithful to Him, He will provide for our needs; if we are faithful with a little, He will entrust us with more. Being rich in money is not the most important thing. If our children grow up to love the Lord and do well in life, how much wealthier could we be? If we have a successful marriage characterized by mutual love and respect, how much wealthier could we be? If we enjoy continuing and growing intimacy with God, how much wealthier could we be? Material prosperity may come, but that is not the ultimate goal. We must learn to think as God thinks, to value what He values, and to lay up treasures for ourselves in Heaven. True prosperity comes only from the Lord. The wealth of God works from the inside out. *Effective churches enjoy the wealth of God.*

Not Against Flesh and Blood

Finally, after they have been restored and are walking in each of the first six habits, effective churches practice the seventh habit of *waging warfare under God*. Once we get serious about God and about living for Him and doing His will and His work, the enemy will come along and try to tear down and destroy what we are building. The six habits prepare and equip us for waging war against our enemy. It is important that we understand the true nature of that enemy. The apostle Paul may have expressed it best when he wrote:

> *Finally, my brethren, be strong in the Lord and in the power of His might. Put on the whole armor of God, that you may be able to stand against the wiles of the devil. For we do not wrestle against flesh and blood, but against principalities, against powers, against the rulers of the darkness of this age, against spiritual hosts of wickedness in the heavenly places. Therefore take up the whole armor of God, that you may be able to withstand in the evil day, and having done all, to stand* (Ephesians 6:10-13).

Our warfare is not only defensive in nature. For many years, many churches have displayed an attitude of simply trying to "hold the fort" against the devil until Jesus comes to take them home. That approach gives the devil too much credit. Our warfare is to be offensive as well as defensive in nature. It is about aggressively moving out to restore the house of God and see the glory of the Lord fill the earth. We are not here to take *sides*; we are here to take *over!*

God is restoring the Church and calling us to move out with aggression. We are not to be passive any longer. Instead, we are to storm the very gates of hell itself and take back that which the enemy has stolen from us. That means taking back our families, our schools, our streets, our cities, and our nation. This doesn't mean disrespecting other peoples' faith, but it *does* mean affirming our own without apology or compromise. *Effective churches engage in the warfare of God.*

Our warfare is for the purpose not only of protection, but also of *penetration*. It means launching out aggressively into the world and claiming it for God! That's why the house of God *must* be restored! We are God's second wave of assault troops attacking the enemy's lines. Jesus was the first. A restored house is part of God's strategy for the ages to bring in His harvest and release His glory throughout the earth! *O Lord, let it come! Let it come, Lord Jesus!*

CHAPTER TEN

The House Restored

When the Lord sets out to restore His house, nothing will stop Him from completing the work. God is faithful; He will finish what He starts. God is true; He will fulfill all His promises. Not a single one will be left undone. The Old Testament Book of Ezra gives us encouragement as we see how God restored His house among the Jews returning from the Babylonian exile.

After 70 years of forced exile, the Jews were returning home. King Cyrus, whose Persian Empire had supplanted the Babylonians, had released the Jews to return to their homeland and rebuild the temple in Jerusalem. Can you imagine what it must have been like for them as they approached the city? Only the very oldest in the group could remember the "old days," the days of horror and terror when Jerusalem and the entire land of Judah had been under attack. The younger ones had undoubtedly heard the stories many times. God's judgment had fallen on the people because they had turned away from Him and followed false gods. Jerusalem had been destroyed by the Babylonian army and the walls of the city had been torn down. Worse still, the temple, the beautiful temple of Solomon that Josiah had restored, was in ruins!

Once the people arrived in the city, they lost no time getting started. The people of God had returned to the land. *God was restoring His house!*

> *From the first day of the seventh month they began to offer burnt offerings to the Lord, although the foundation of the temple of the Lord had not been laid....When the builders laid the foundation of the temple of the Lord, the priests stood in their apparel with trumpets, and the Levites, the sons of Asaph, with cymbals, to praise the Lord, according to the ordinance of David king of Israel. And they sang responsively, praising and giving thanks to the Lord: "For He is good, for His mercy endures forever toward Israel." Then all the people shouted with a great shout, when they praised the Lord, because the foundation of the house of the Lord was laid. But many of the priests and Levites and heads of the fathers' houses, old men who had seen the first temple, wept with a loud voice when the foundation of this temple was laid before their eyes. Yet many shouted aloud for joy, so that the people could not discern the noise of the shout of joy from the noise of the weeping of the people, for the people shouted with a loud shout, and the sound was heard afar off* (Ezra 3:6,10-13).

Even before the foundation for the new temple was laid, the priests began offering burnt sacrifices at the site. The people celebrated with trumpets, cymbals, singing, praise, thanksgiving, and shouting so great that it was heard "afar off"; and this was just at the laying of the foundation! Imagine the scene that would take place when the temple was completed! *God was restoring His house!*

Delayed but Not Defeated

It wasn't long before trouble popped up. The non-Jewish occupants of the land and the surrounding regions, many of whom had rejoiced at the destruction of the nation of Judah, were not happy to see the Jews return. They were particularly upset that the temple was being rebuilt.

Then the people of the land tried to discourage the people of Judah. They troubled them in building, and hired counselors against them to frustrate their purpose all the days of Cyrus king of Persia, even until the reign of Darius king of Persia. In the reign of Ahasuerus, in the beginning of his reign, they wrote an accusation against the inhabitants of Judah and Jerusalem (Ezra 4:4-6).

Enemies of God will always oppose efforts to restore God's house, either openly or behind the scenes. Some are easier to spot than others. The most difficult ones to identify are often the closest, because they hide behind the cloak of religion and mingle with the rest of us in our churches! These are the ones who are always against anything that will help the church grow, or who are at the center of contention and controversy. We must be very careful here. Not everyone in the church who disagrees with us or who opposes new ideas or ministries or the like is an enemy of God. Genuine believers who love the Lord often have genuine, honest differences of opinion. The key is careful, diligent prayer and sensitivity to the Holy Spirit in order to arrive at a mutual understanding of what the Lord wants. We can know each other by our fruits. Eventually, the true enemies of God among us will reveal themselves. The Lord will expose them.

Initially, the adversaries of the temple project had asked to take part with the Jews in the building (see Ezra 4:1-2). When their request was refused, their hostility came out into the open. When their letter to Ahasuerus apparently did not produce the desired result, they sent another letter to Artaxerxes, the new king. This letter contained a negative and inflammatory account of the Jews and their activities with regard to the temple, designed to cause the king to see the project as a political threat and to stop it. The plot worked. Artaxerxes issued a letter commanding that all work on the temple cease until he gave permission for it to resume.

Now when the copy of King Artaxerxes' letter was read before Rehum, Shimshai the scribe, and their companions, they went up in haste to Jerusalem against the Jews, and by force of arms made them cease. Thus the work of the house of God which is at Jerusalem ceased, and it was discontinued until the second year of the reign of Darius king of Persia (Ezra 4:23-24).

Sometimes opposition from the world can delay the fulfillment of God's plan and purpose, but it can never defeat or destroy them. God is sovereign and His purpose will be accomplished. Everything that the Lord has said He will do, *He will do!* Even during this time, God's purpose was underway. *God was restoring His house!*

Purpose Fulfilled

Work on the temple lapsed for about 25 years. Then the Lord stirred the hearts of His people again.

Then the prophet Haggai and Zechariah the son of Iddo, prophets, prophesied to the Jews who were in Judah and Jerusalem, in the name of the God of Israel, who was over them. So Zerubbabel the son of Shealtiel and Jeshua the son of Jozadak rose up and began to build the house of God which is in Jerusalem; and the prophets of God were with them, helping them (Ezra 5:1-2).

Notice that when work on the temple resumed, the prophets Haggai and Zechariah were involved, helping with the building and encouraging the work with words from the Lord. As before, opponents of the work sought to stop it. Tattenai, the governor of the region, sent a letter to the new king, Darius, asking for verification of a report given him by the Jews that King Cyrus had authorized and decreed the rebuilding of the temple. Darius searched the royal archives, confirmed the existence of Cyrus's decree, and sent a reply to Tattenai, ordering him to render any assistance needed in helping the Jews finish the temple. God's purpose could not be stayed! *God was restoring His house!*

Now the temple was finished on the third day of the month of Adar, which was in the sixth year of the reign of King Darius.

Then the children of Israel, the priests and the Levites and the rest of the descendants of the captivity, celebrated the dedication of this house of God with joy. And they offered sacrifices at the dedication of this house of God, one hundred bulls, two hundred rams, four hundred lambs, and as a sin offering for all Israel twelve male goats, according to the number of the tribes of Israel. They assigned the priests to their divisions and the Levites to their divisions, over the service of God in Jerusalem, as it is written in the Book of Moses. And the descendants of the captivity kept the Passover on the fourteenth day of the first month. For the priests and the Levites had purified themselves; all of them were ritually clean. And they slaughtered the Passover lambs for all the descendants of the captivity, for their brethren the priests, and for themselves. Then the children of Israel who had returned from the captivity ate together with all who had separated themselves from the filth of the nations of the land in order to seek the Lord God of Israel. And they kept the Feast of Unleavened Bread seven days with joy; for the Lord made them joyful, and turned the heart of the king of Assyria toward them, to strengthen their hands in the work of the house of God, the God of Israel (Ezra 6:15-22).

The completion of the temple was a cause for great joy among the returned exiles. The dedication service alone involved the sacrifice of 512 animals, and was certainly a day that was remembered always by everyone who participated. Later, as in the days of Josiah, the people celebrated a magnificent and joyous Passover, probably the first one in 70 years or longer. God brought all of this about, and filled His people with joy. He had turned the heart of a pagan king to look favorably upon them. In faithfulness to His promises, the Lord had redeemed His people and brought them back to their homeland. Under His guiding hand and by His sustaining grace and power, they had rebuilt the temple of the Lord. *God had restored His house!*

A New Thing

I n this day we are living in, at the dawn of a new millennium, God is restoring His house. Because God is creative by nature, it should not surprise us that He is always doing new things, or doing established things in new ways. Yet so many of us resist change. We would much rather stay with the established and the familiar. That's why we so often get uncomfortable when God begins to prod us and nudge us in new directions. That's also why many times the people who were the most active in a *previous* move of God are the greatest opponents of a *current* move of God. In Ezra 3:12, many of the priests, Levites, and old men who could remember the first temple wept at sight of the foundation of the new one. Perhaps this was because the new temple would not be as large or as splendid as Solomon's temple. Perhaps they remembered the "old days" and were reluctant to move into a new era. They wanted things to be as they once were.

The Lord wants us to be ready to move in new directions and do new things. We can't experience restoration or enter into the full realization of His purpose otherwise. Listen to what He is saying to us:

> *Do not remember the former things, nor consider the things of old. Behold, I will do a new thing, now it shall spring forth; shall you not know it? I will even make a road in the wilderness and rivers in the desert. The beast of the field will honor Me, the jackals and the ostriches, because I give waters in the wilderness and rivers in the desert, to give drink to My people, My chosen. This people I have formed for Myself; they shall declare My praise* (Isaiah 43:18-21).

It's time to forget the old things. God is doing a new thing! "Waters in the wilderness and rivers in the desert" are pictures of *restoration*. The people of God drink of this water and are renewed, refreshed, and restored.

> *Behold, the days are coming, says the Lord, when I will make a new covenant with the house of Israel and with the house of Judah; not according to the covenant that I made with their*

fathers in the day that I took them by the hand to lead them out of the land of Egypt, My covenant which they broke, though I was a husband to them, says the Lord. But this is the covenant that I will make with the house of Israel after those days, says the Lord: I will put My law in their minds, and write it on their hearts; and I will be their God, and they shall be My people. No more shall every man teach his neighbor, and every man his brother, saying, "Know the Lord," for they all shall know Me, from the least of them to the greatest of them, says the Lord. For I will forgive their iniquity, and their sin I will remember no more (Jeremiah 31:31-34).

This is another promise of restoration. Again, God is doing something new! Commenting on these verses, the writer of Hebrews says, "In that He says, 'A new covenant,' He has made the first obsolete. Now what is becoming obsolete and growing old is ready to vanish away" (Heb. 8:13). The old must pass away before the new can come. In God's restored house, *everyone* knows Him, "from the least of them to the greatest of them," and His law is implanted in their minds and written on their hearts.

Jesus also stressed the importance of being open to the new things that God does.

"No one puts a piece of unshrunk cloth on an old garment; for the patch pulls away from the garment, and the tear is made worse. Nor do they put new wine into old wineskins, or else the wineskins break, the wine is spilled, and the wineskins are ruined. But they put new wine into new wineskins, and both are preserved" (Matthew 9:16-17).

God is busy pouring new wine. The question is, what kind of wineskins are we—old or *new*? Get ready! The Lord is doing a new thing! *God is restoring His house!*

God's House Restored

Around the world today an unprecedented movement of the Spirit of God is underway in the Church—a movement of a like unseen since the first century. The fields of the world are white, and God is restoring His house to receive the harvest. The grain is ready for reaping, and Christ is restoring His Church and sending workers into the fields. We are the workers. The fields are our families and friends, our streets and neighborhoods, our schools and workplaces, our cities and seats of government. They are the country clubs and the crack houses, the barrooms and the brothels, the prisons and the palaces.

God is restoring His house. The question is, *are we ready?*

God is moving all things toward the day when the vision revealed to John will be fulfilled:

> *Now I saw a new heaven and a new earth, for the first heaven and the first earth had passed away. Also there was no more sea. Then I, John, saw the holy city, New Jerusalem, coming down out of heaven from God, prepared as a bride adorned for her husband. And I heard a loud voice from heaven saying, "Behold, the tabernacle of God is with men, and He will dwell with them, and they shall be His people. God Himself will be with them and be their God. And God will wipe away every tear from their eyes; there shall be no more death, nor sorrow, nor crying. There shall be no more pain, for the former things have passed away." Then He who sat on the throne said, "Behold, I make all things new." And He said to me, "Write, for these words are true and faithful"* (Revelation 21:1-5).

God is restoring His house to be a bride, pure and without spot, wrinkle, or blemish, adorned in beauty and holiness for His Son, the Bridegroom. Behold, He has made all things new! Amen, so be it! *Lord, we stand ready! Bring Your great harvest home! O Lord, restore Your house!*

Other
Destiny Image titles
you will enjoy reading

THE LOST PASSIONS OF JESUS
by Donald L. Milam, Jr.

What motivated Jesus to pursue the cross? What inner strength kept His feet on the path laid before Him? Time and tradition have muted the Church's knowledge of the passions that burned in Jesus' heart, but if we want to—if we dare to—we can still seek those same passions. Learn from a close look at Jesus' own life and words and from the writings of other dedicated followers the passions that enflamed the Son of God and changed the world forever!

ISBN 0-9677402-0-7

THE ASCENDED LIFE
by Bernita J. Conway.

A believer does not need to wait until Heaven to experience an intimate relationship with the Lord. When you are born again, your life becomes His, and He pours His life into yours. Here Bernita Conway explains from personal study and experience the truth of "abiding in the Vine," the Lord Jesus Christ. When you grasp this understanding and begin to walk in it, it will change your whole life and relationship with your heavenly Father!

ISBN 1-56043-337-X

THE MARTYRS' TORCH
by Bruce Porter.

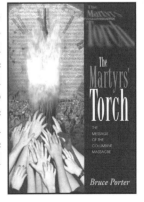

In every age of history, darkness has threatened to extinguish the light. But also in every age of history, heroes and heroines of the faith rose up to hold high the torch of their testimony—witnesses to the truth of the gospel of Jesus Christ. On a fateful spring day at Columbine High, others lifted up their torches and joined the crimson path of the martyrs' way. We cannot forget their sacrifice. A call is sounding forth from Heaven: "Who will take up the martyrs' torch which fell from these faithful hands?" Will you?

ISBN 0-7684-2046-6

Available at your local Christian bookstore.

Internet: http://www.reapernet.com

Other
Destiny Image *titles*
you will enjoy reading

GOD'S FAVORITE HOUSE
by Tommy Tenney.
The burning desire of your heart can be fulfilled. God is looking for people just like you. He is a Lover in search of a people who will love Him in return. He is far more interested in you than He is interested in a building. He would hush all of Heaven's hosts to listen to your voice raised in heartfelt love songs to Him. This book will show you how to build a house of worship within, fulfilling your heart's desire and His!
ISBN 0-7684-2043-1

THE GOD CHASERS (Best-selling **Destiny Image** book)
by Tommy Tenney.
There are those so hungry, so desperate for His presence, that they become consumed with finding Him. Their longing for Him moves them to do what they would otherwise never do: Chase God. But what does it really mean to chase God? Can He be "caught"? Is there an end to the thirsting of man's soul for Him? Meet Tommy Tenney—God chaser. Join him in his search for God. Follow him as he ignores the maze of religious tradition and finds himself, not chasing God, but to his utter amazement, caught by the One he had chased.
ISBN 0-7684-2016-4

GOD CHASERS DAILY MEDITATION & PERSONAL JOURNAL
by Tommy Tenney.
Does your heart yearn to have an intimate relationship with your Lord? Perhaps you long to draw closer to your heavenly Father, but you don't know how or where to start. This *Daily Meditation & Personal Journal* will help you begin a journey that will change your life. As you read and journal, you'll find your spirit running to meet Him with a desire and fervor you've never before experienced. Let your heart hunger propel you into the chase of your life...after God!
ISBN 0-7684-2040-7

HIDDEN TREASURES OF THE HEART
by Donald Downing.
What is hidden in your heart? Your heart is the key to life—both natural and spiritual. If you aren't careful with your heart, you run the risk of becoming vulnerable to the attacks of the enemy. This book explains the changes you need to make to ensure that your commitment to God is from the heart and encourages you to make those changes. Don't miss out on the greatest blessing of all—a clean heart!
ISBN 1-56043-315-9

Available at your local Christian bookstore.

Internet: http://www.reapernet.com

Other Destiny Image *titles* you will enjoy reading

AN INVITATION TO FRIENDSHIP: From the Father's Heart, Volume 2
by Charles Slagle.
Our God is a Father whose heart longs for His children to sit and talk with Him in fellowship and oneness. This second volume of intimate letters from the Father to you, His child, reveals His passion, dreams, and love for you. As you read them, you will find yourself drawn ever closer within the circle of His embrace. The touch of His presence will change your life forever!
ISBN 0-7684-2013-X

FATHER, FORGIVE US!
by Jim W. Goll.
What is holding back a worldwide "great awakening"? What hinders the Church all over the world from rising up and bringing in the greatest harvest ever known? The answer is simple: sin! God is calling Christians today to take up the mantle of identificational intercession and repent for the sins of the present and past; for the sins of our fathers; for the sins of the nations. Will you heed the call? This book shows you how!
ISBN 0-7684-2025-3

THE COSTLY ANOINTING
by Lori Wilke.
In this book, teacher and prophetic songwriter Lori Wilke boldly reveals God's requirements for being entrusted with an awesome power and authority. She speaks directly from God's heart to your heart concerning the most costly anointing. This is a word that will change your life!
ISBN 1-56043-051-6

NAKED AND NOT ASHAMED
by T.D. Jakes.
With a powerful anointing, Bishop T.D. Jakes challenges us to go below the surface and become completely and honestly vulnerable before God and man. In relationships, in prayer, in ministry—we need to be willing to be open and transparent. Why do we fear? God already knows us, but He cannot heal our hidden hurts unless we expose them to Him. Only then can we be *Naked and Not Ashamed*!
ISBN 1-56043-835-5

Available at your local Christian bookstore.

Internet: http://www.reapernet.com

Other
*Destiny Image **titles***
you will enjoy reading

THE LOST ART OF INTERCESSION
by Jim W. Goll.
Finally there is something that really explains what is happening to so many folk in the Body of Christ. What does it mean to carry the burden of the Lord? Where is it in Scripture and in history? Why do I feel as though God is groaning within me? No, you are not crazy; God is restoring genuine intercessory prayer in the hearts of those who are open to respond to His burden and His passion.
ISBN 1-56043-697-2

THE HIDDEN POWER OF PRAYER AND FASTING
by Mahesh Chavda.
The praying believer is the confident believer. But the fasting believer is the over-coming believer. This is the believer who changes the circumstances and the world around him. He is the one who experiences the supernatural power of the risen Lord in his everyday life. An international evangelist and the senior pastor of All Nations Church in Charlotte, North Carolina, Mahesh Chavda has seen firsthand the power of God released through a lifestyle of prayer and fasting. Here he shares from decades of personal experience and scriptural study principles and practical tips about fasting and praying. This book will inspire you to tap into God's power and change your life, your city, and your nation!
ISBN 0-7684-2017-2

ENCOUNTERING THE PRESENCE
by Colin Urquhart.
What is it about Jesus that, when we encounter Him, we are changed? When we encounter the Presence, we encounter the Truth, because Jesus is the Truth. Here Colin Urquhart, best-selling author and pastor in Sussex, England, explains how the Truth changes facts. Do you desire to become more like Jesus? The Truth will set you free!
ISBN 0-7684-2018-0

THE MORE EXCELLENT MINISTRY
by Kelley Varner.
In *The More Excellent Ministry* Pastor Varner shows you where God's fullness flows unhindered and how you can walk in it.
ISBN 0-914903-60-8

Available at your local Christian bookstore.

Internet: http://www.reapernet.com

Exciting titles
by Don Nori

Other
Destiny Image titles
you will enjoy reading

LADY IN WAITING
by Debby Jones and Jackie Kendall.
This is not just another book for single women! The authors, both well-known conference speakers, present an in-depth study on the biblical Ruth that reveals the characteristics every woman of God should develop. Learn how you can become a lady of faith, purity, contentment, patience—and much more—as you pursue a personal and intimate relationship with your Lord Jesus!
ISBN 1-56043-848-7
Devotional Journal and Study Guide
ISBN 1-56043-298-5

YOU CAN BE THE HAPPY MOM OF AN EMPTY NEST
by Darien B. Cooper.
In-laws, "out-laws," and elderly parents—is your family a dream come true or one of your worst nightmares? Here Darien Cooper, author of the best-selling *You Can Be the Wife of a Happy Husband*, tells how to be the happy mom of an empty nest. A wife, mother, and grandmother, she shares three principles that will help make your relationship with your family happier and more enjoyable. You can turn that nightmare into a "dream come true"!
ISBN 1-56043-333-7

DON'T DIE IN THE WINTER...
by Dr. Millicent Thompson.
Why do we go through hard times? Why must we suffer pain? In *Don't Die in the Winter...* Dr. Thompson, a pastor, teacher, and conference speaker, explains the spiritual seasons and cycles that people experience. A spiritual winter is simply a season that tests our growth. We need to endure our winters, for in the plan of God, spring always follows winter!
ISBN 1-56043-558-5

THE MIRACLE OF THE SCARLET THREAD
by Richard Booker.
From Genesis to Revelation, the scarlet thread is woven through every book of the Bible. This Richard Booker classic provides a new way to unravel the complexities of the Bible to give us a better overview of God's perfect planning.
ISBN 0-914903-26-8

Available at your local Christian bookstore.

Internet: http://www.reapernet.com

Other
*Destiny Image **titles***
you will enjoy reading

NO MORE SOUR GRAPES
by Don Nori.
Who among us wants our children to be free from the struggles we have had to bear? Who among us wants the lives of our children to be full of victory and love for their Lord? Who among us wants the hard-earned lessons from our lives given freely to our children? All these are not only possible, they are also God's will. You can be one of those who share the excitement and joy of seeing your children step into the destiny God has for them. If you answered "yes" to these questions, the pages of this book are full of hope and help for you and others just like you.
ISBN 0-7684-2037-7

SOLDIERS WITH LITTLE FEET
by Dian Layton.
Every time God pours out His Spirit, the adult generation moves on without its children. Dian pleads with the Church to bring the children into the fullness of God with them and offers practical guidelines for doing so.
ISBN 0-914903-86-1

THE BATTLE FOR THE SEED
by Dr. Patricia Morgan.
The dilemma facing young people today is a major concern for all parents. This important book shows God's way to change the condition of the young and advance God's purpose for every nation into the next century.
ISBN 1-56043-099-0

CHILDREN OF REVIVAL
by Vann Lane.
What do you do with hundreds of children during services that last for hours? At first Pastor Vann Lane thought he would use all his usual "stuff" to entertain the children. The Lord thought differently. In this book you'll read remarkable stories of Brownsville Assembly's 11-year-old leader, the worship band of young musicians, and the 75-member prayer team of children between ages 8 and 12 years old. *Children of Revival* will forever change the way you view the Church's little members.
ISBN 1-56043-699-9

IT'S TIME
by Richard Crisco.
"We say that 'Generation X' does not know what they are searching for in life. But we are wrong. They know what they desire. We, as the Church, are the ones without a revelation of what they need." It is time to stop entertaining our youth with pizza parties and start training an army for God. Find out in this dynamic book how the Brownsville youth have exploded with revival power...affecting the surrounding schools and communities!
ISBN 1-56043-690-5

Available at your local Christian bookstore.

Internet: http://www.reapernet.com

Other
Destiny Image titles
you will enjoy reading

NON-RELIGIOUS CHRISTIANITY
by Gerald Coates.
If Jesus Christ returned today, how much of "church" would He condone or condemn? In this book, Gerald Coates contends that "religion" is the greatest hindrance to making Jesus attractive to our family, neighbors, and co-workers. Humorous yet confrontational, this popular British speaker and church leader will surprise you with his conclusions. This book could change your life forever!
ISBN 1-56043-694-8

THE RADICAL CHURCH
by Bryn Jones.
The world of the apostles and the world of today may look a lot different, but there is one thing that has not changed: the need for a radical Church in a degenerate society. We still need a church, a body of people, who will bring a hard-hitting, totally unfamiliar message: Jesus has come to set us free! Bryn Jones of Ansty, Coventry, United Kingdom, an apostolic leader to numerous churches across the world, will challenge your view of what church is and what it is not. Be prepared to learn afresh of the Church that Jesus Christ is building today!
ISBN 0-7684-2022-9

THE RELEASE OF THE HUMAN SPIRIT
by Frank Houston.
Your relationship and walk with the Lord will only go as deep as your spirit is free. Many things "contain" people and keep them in a box—old traditions, wrong thinking, religious mind-sets, emotional hurts, bitterness—the list is endless. A New Zealander by birth and a naturalized Australian citizen, Frank Houston has been jumping out of those "boxes" all his life. For more than 50 years he has been busy living in revival and fulfilling his God-given destiny, regardless of what other people—or even himself—thinks! In this book you'll discover what it takes to "break out" and find release in the fullness of your Lord. The joy and fulfillment that you will experience will catapult you into a greater and fuller level of living!
ISBN 0-7684-2019-9

ANOINTED OR ANNOYING?
by Ken Gott.
Don't miss out on the powerful move of God that is in the earth today! When you encounter God's Presence in revival, you have a choice—accept it or reject it; become anointed or annoying! Ken Gott, former pastor of Sunderland Christian Centre and now head of Revival Now! International Ministries, calls you to examine your own heart and motives for pursuing God's anointing, and challenges you to walk a life of obedience!
ISBN 0-7684-1003-7

Available at your local Christian bookstore.

Internet: http://www.reapernet.com